Bibliographic information published by the German National Library:

The German National Library lists this publication in the National Bibliography; detailed bibliographic data are available on the Internet at http://dnb.dnb.de .

Imprint:

Copyright © 2013 GRIN Verlag, Open Publishing GmbH
Print and binding: Books on Demand GmbH, Norderstedt Germany
ISBN: 978-3-668-10360-3

This book at GRIN:

http://www.grin.com/en/e-book/311374/speech-as-interface-in-web-applications-for-visually-challenged

Prabhat Verma

Speech as Interface in Web Applications for Visually Challenged

GRIN Publishing

GRIN - Your knowledge has value

Since its foundation in 1998, GRIN has specialized in publishing academic texts by students, college teachers and other academics as e-book and printed book. The website www.grin.com is an ideal platform for presenting term papers, final papers, scientific essays, dissertations and specialist books.

Visit us on the internet:

http://www.grin.com/

http://www.facebook.com/grincom

http://www.twitter.com/grin_com

SPEECH AS INTERFACE IN WEB-APPLICATIONS FOR VISUALLY CHALLENGED

**A Thesis Submitted
In Partial Fulfillment of Requirements
for the degree of**

DOCTOR OF PHILOSOPHY

by

PRABHAT VERMA
(Enrollment No. 09001001013)

**Under the Supervision of
PROF. RAGHURAJ SINGH**
Harcourt Butler Technological Institute, Kanpur -208002. India.

to the
FACULTY OF COMPUTER SCIENCE AND ENGINEERING
UTTARAKHAND TECHNICAL UNIVERSITY
D E H R A D U N
November, 2012

CERTIFICATE

Certified that **Mr. Prabhat Verma** (**Enrollment No. 09001001013**) has carried out the research work presented in this thesis entitled **"Speech as Interface in Web Applications for Visually Challenged"** for the award of **Doctor of Philosophy** from Uttarakhand Technical University, Dehradun under my supervision. The thesis embodies results of original work, and studies are carried out by the student himself and the contents of the thesis do not form the basis for the award of any other degree to the candidate or to anybody else from this or any other University/Institution.

(Dr. Raghuraj Singh)
Professor
Harcourt Butler Technological Institute,
Kanpur (Uttar Pradesh). India.

Date:

ABSTRACT

This research work addresses to some of the important issues related to web accessibility in context of visually challenged users. Accessibility refers to the ability of a user, despite disabilities or impairments, to use a resource. For Internet-based applications, accessibility means that all users can perceive, understand, navigate, interact with, and contribute to the Web. Speech is a convenient medium of interaction for visually challenged users, Internet accessibility for them is made possible by providing an alternative speech-based interface for human-computer interaction.

Problems associated with speech based web interfaces are manifold. Most of the web content available today has been designed for the visual interface via graphical browsers. Sighted individuals can quickly locate the information that is most relevant to them. Visual layout of the webpage also helps a lot in efficient browsing of the webpage. But, this task can be time consuming and extremely difficult for people with visual disabilities. Speech based browsers are generally sequential in processing. Thus, a visually challenged user may require 'listening' the whole page content in order to reach his/her topic of interest. Also, they are not able to get any layout information of the web page.

Assistive Technologies (ATs) like screen readers make the use of underlying DOM (Document Object Model) structure of the web page to narrate its contents to a visually challenged user. To ensure that ATs work correctly on a webpage, web developers must follow the W3C and other guidelines while creating the websites. Unfortunately, due to lack of awareness among web developers, this requirement is not adequately met and as a result, a large amount of web content remains inaccessible to ATs and visually challenged users. Web 2.0 has further increased this trend by empowering the end user with web authoring capabilities. The role of ATs is thus to expose such inaccessible webpage contents using some clever techniques and present them before the visually challenged user.

Despite their shortcomings, Screen Readers have been the primary tool for using internet by visually challenged. Unfortunately, most of the popular and workable screen readers are proprietary and bear a heavy price tag. For example, cost of JAWS, a popular screen reader by Freedom Scientific for single user license is around $900. This cost is 10 times higher than that of Windows7 operating system! The cost is evidently too high to be afforded by an average Indian individual with visual disability. High cost is also attributed by small product market for assistive tools. There are ATs in freeware domain but they are not popular since most of them may not provide adequate functionalities.

ATs for web access pose greater problems as compare to ATs for Desktop Applications. *Microsoft Narrator* integrated in Windows 7 Operating System works only for Desktop Applications and not for web access. Findings of a study conducted by Enabling Dimensions, January 2002, New Delhi, reveal that accessing web content was "frustratingly difficult" for visually challenged, implying the need for availability of more accessible and usable web content as well as better software to use the Web effectively by them. Thus, design and develop of usable as well as affordable assistive tools for visually challenged users is an important research issue.

In confirmation to the *"Research by Application Development"* philosophy adopted and as a part of this research work, an enhanced speech based web browser named *'WACTA'* has been designed and developed with a vision of providing an improved yet affordable and easy to use web browser for visually challenged users. The system has been implemented in programming language C# and .NET 4.0 framework. Microsoft Speech API (SAPI 5.0) has been used for narration of the text and user input feedback.

WACTA web Browser has several unique features that distinct it from other screen readers. First, the speech based web browser has been implemented completely using .NET managed code. So far, screen readers have been implemented using unmanaged code (Ihtml interface). Implementation in managed code offers better reliability, automatic garbage collection, bounds checking at run-time, improved security etc. Due to limited available functionalities, coding in C# managed code poses greater challenges in ensuring the requisite behavior of ATs. Second, speech features have been integrated in the WACTA browser itself which is implemented using WebBrowser class. Thus, the web browser can be customized for visually challenged users and new functionalities can be added later. It can be used in many modes depending upon the user need and user disability level. Thus, there are link navigation mode, navigate-all mode, interactive mode, newsreader mode, query mode, analytical mode and mouse Glimpse mode (for partially blind user) which can be chosen from among menu or using the key shortcuts. At any time, visually challenged user can make switch over from one mode to another. It aids to minimizing the time required to complete a given task. WACTA complies with the W3C's User Agent Accessibility Guidelines (UAAG). The prototype is already tested for 25 skilled blind users and they have found it user friendly as it fulfills their basic requirements to access the internet effectively for both routine and important tasks.

There are important tasks like getting a berth booked on Railways Reservation Website, paying taxes at Income tax website etc. which are complex in nature and have span about multiple web pages. Such task may not be conveniently performed by a visually challenged user with the aid of assistive technologies like screen readers. Besides, the assistive tools may not be installed on a public terminal. This makes a disadvantage for visually challenged users since the web based facility to utilize these public utilities is even more needed for them than their visually able counterparts. Such important public utilities should be universally accessible without the need to install any assistive tool on the computer used. At present, fetching mp3 on a remote web service is the only standard way for converting text to speech. APIs used for this purpose are proprietary and provide text to speech services. In this context, we have proposed two frameworks using which, owners of the public utility websites may directly speech enables their existing websites for more important functionalities at a minimum cost and effort required. The first framework, Speech-Enabler makes use of existing technologies like JavaScript and speech API, therefore provides robust and lightweight solution to the accessibility problem. The other framework, SICE Framework is based on VoiceXML and Voice-Over Internet Protocol (VOIP). It can be used for developing web based interactive voice applications without the need of telephony. Thus, complex web data can be conveniently handled using customized two way dialogue based access system in a controlled way.

To the best of our knowledge, at present no formal framework is available to evaluate the performance of assistive tools in quantitative terms that are used by visually challenged users to use internet. This research work takes some initiative in this direction by formulating a hierarchical model for quantitative evaluation of assistive tools for blinds. Identifying various Performance Attributes and Usage Metrics, we have established relationship among these to obtain the Overall Performance Index of the assistive tools.

This research work has strengthened our belief that knowledge and technology should be used in favor of mankind to every possible extent. Internet is a wonderful tool having ability to compensate the visual impairment with technology. Design and development of powerful yet affordable speech-based interfaces would be certainly helpful in enhancing the overall Quality of Life of visually challenged. The work done by us shall be further taken up in future e.g. enhancing the features and capabilities of WACTA web browser, its design and development for Android based Tablet Computers as well as extending it for Hindi scripted websites.

ACKNOWLEDGEMENT

I would like to express my deepest gratitude to my Supervisor, **Prof. Raghuraj Singh** for his guidance and support throughout this research work. His single mindedness, dedication and enthusiasm towards research have constantly inspired me. It has been an honor working with him.

I am thankful to Uttarakhand Technical University, Dehradun for providing me the opportunity and approval to do this research work.

This research is a part of the Major Research Project entitled "Design and Development of Web Browser for Visually Challenged" funded by the University Grants Commission, New Delhi running in Computer Science & Engineering Department of Harcourt Butler Technological Institute, Kanpur during the year 2009 - 2012. I would like to thank the University Grant Commission, New Delhi for extending all the support to realize this work.

I am thankful to Harcourt Butler Technological Institute, Kanpur for providing necessary facilities to complete this research work.

I am thankful to Adult Training Centre, National Institute of Visually Handicap, Dehradun for providing their help and support for the research work.

I am greatly indebted to Prof. Padam Kumar, Professor and Head, Department of Electronics and Computer Engineering, Indian Institute of Technology, Roorkee for his valuable suggestions regarding the principles of good research work.

I am thankful to Prof. Hema A Murthi, Indian Institute of Technology, Chennai for her valuable suggestions regarding the scope of this research work at the very beginning.

Finally, I am thankful to my family members, friends, and colleagues for supporting me directly or indirectly in this work.

(Prabhat Verma)

TABLE OF CONTENTS

PART ONE

(Introduction, Literature Survey, Problem Identification and Issues)

PART TWO

(Problem Solutions, Approaches and Methodologies)

PART THREE

**(Results and Findings, Discussion, Conclusions
and Directions for Future Research)**

LIST OF TABLES

LIST OF FIGURES

CHAPTER 1
INTRODUCTION

One of the original goals of the proponents of internet was to provide equal access to information for all irrespective of their disabilities. The idea was to represent documents on different platforms and different user interfaces including text-based and auditory interfaces in a single computer network. It was then planned to convert each document into Braille [1]. After a success story of more than two decades of Internet, this goal is still only partially met. Findings of a study conducted by Enabling Dimensions, January 2002, New Delhi, reveal that accessing web content was "frustratingly difficult" for visually challenged, implying the need for availability of more accessible and usable web content as well as better software to use the Web effectively by them[2]. Internet technology can become a very effective tool for visually challenged in compensating their disability by empowering them with the knowledge and information of choices available as regards employment, independent living etc [3].

The web has become an indispensable source of information and we use it for performing routine tasks as well. The primary mode of interaction with the web is via graphical browsers, which are designed for visual interaction. As we browse the Web, we have to filter through a lot of irrelevant data. Sighted individuals can process visual data in no time at all. They can quickly locate the information that is most relevant to them. Visual layout of the webpage also helps a lot in efficient browsing of the webpage. But, this task can be time consuming and extremely difficult for people with visual disabilities. They are not able to get any layout information of the web page. Speech based browsers are generally sequential in processing. Therefore, clever techniques must be applied for presenting the items available on the website as per the need of the user.

Despite their shortcomings, Screen Readers have been the primary tool for using internet by visually challenged. Costs of major commercial Screen Readers are not trivial at present which is clear from the following data [4]:

- JAWS (Standard)   Single User License: $895.
- Window-Eyes   Single User License: $895.
- HAL   Single User License: $795.
- System Access   Single User License: $399.

The cost is evidently too high to be afforded by an average Indian individual with visual disability. This cost is 10 times higher than that of Windows7 Operating System! High cost is also attributed by small product market for assistive tools. Thus, there is a need to design and develop usable as well as affordable assistive tools for visually challenged users.

1.1 MAJOR OBJECTIVES

This research work aims to bring new insights in the broad area of Human-Computer Interaction from the view point of visually challenged people. Major objectives of this research are as given below:

- To study and analyze the existing systems of Web browsing for visually challenged and to identify enhancement possibilities.
- To devise the most plausible way of text surfing, searching, querying, Information/data extraction, Form–Filling, mailing, blogging etc. in view of the constraints of visually challenged Users.
- To design and develop the Speech based Browsing System for above usages.
- To formulate a framework for the Performance Evaluation of Speech based Browsing Systems.

1.2 DOMAIN OF THE RESEARCH

This research work encompasses the following domain specific tasks or subtasks related to human computer interaction:

i.   Design and development of speech based improved Interfaces,
ii. Web Content Analysis and Management,
iii. Speech based Interactions,
iv. Keyboard based Accessibility.

It must be emphasized that this work makes the use of existing speech technologies only and the domain of speech processing, speech analysis or signal processing is beyond the scope of this research.

1.3 RESEARCH SCOPE

Some of the identified research issues in this domain are as follows:

i.   Finding Scope for enhancement of Accessibility and usability of inaccessible web content using affordable Assistive Technology (AT).
ii. Designing the framework for enhanced Speech based Web Browser/Screen Reader,
iii. Devising better approaches to Intra/Inter Web page Link-Navigation,
iv. Need for direct speech enabled Public Utility Websites for visually challenged users.
v.   Performance Evaluation criteria for Assistive Technology.

1.4 A SURVEY FOR ASSESSMENT OF USER REQUIREMENTS

A Successful design requires an understanding of the target user groups and their goals, requirements, preferences, difficulties with existing systems etc. To get the status and exact requirement of web accessibility & usability among visually disabled, we made a survey with a group of 50 visually disabled at Adult Training Centre, National Institute of Visually Handicap, Dehradun, India. The participants were comfortable in using normal keyboards for providing inputs to the computer. Screen Reader, JAWS was being used by them for web browsing and email. They admired JAWS and admitted that they were able to use internet only because of this software. However, they also told that sometimes they were not able to access all the components of a webpage using JAWS. Most often, they were not able to find where to click on the webpage and as a result not able to proceed further. Thus using JAWS they were able to perform simple tasks e.g. news paper reading, general surfing, knowledge gathering, simple query etc. but they were not comfortable in performing complex tasks involving multiple form filling. Besides, JAWS is not a freeware and its cost is too high to be afforded by an average Indian individual. Thus, the web usage of the participants was limited to the institute laboratory only.

Web usage by a visually disabled user may be categorized into simple, intermediate and complex. A usage is simple if a visually disabled person browses for some news article, e-book or collects information on some topic. Screen Readers may serve well for all such simple usages. Tasks like sending or receiving e-mails, performing simple queries like finding examination result of a student by entering his/her roll number may be considered as of intermediate complexity. Tasks like getting a travel ticket reserved or online shopping are of complex category because they require multiple form filling that may spread across several web pages in a complex structure. Each of the above categories of usage pose different types of issues and challenges for visually disabled, e.g. in the simple category, an intelligent text summarization technique may be helpful to avoid reading from first to last word.

1.5 RESEARCH PROBLEM STATEMENT

"To address the issues and challenges related to Web Accessibility in context of Visually Challenged Internet Users and to devise the most plausible way of using Internet for their important and routine tasks which could empower them to live their life independently with dignity."

3

1.6 PROPOSED SOLUTION

The thesis addresses the core research problem of design, development, implementation and evaluation of an enhanced speech based web browser for visually challenged users. The solution makes the use of keyboard based accessibility through narration of the webpage in a controlled way and by providing speech feedback for user input. Speech features have been integrated in a dedicated web browser itself. Various modes of usages e.g. navigation, interaction, user input, reading, query etc. have been provided with seamless switch over from one mode to another. This makes it possible to quickly locate an element or perform a desired task on web page. The System is implemented using C# and .NET managed code which ensures the requisite robust and error-free operations. WebBrowser class provides skeleton for our web browser. Microsoft Speech API (SAPI 5.1) has been used for speech synthesis. The solution demonstrates the best practice of application design, development and Software Engineering.

On the periphery, we address more general issues related to web accessibility for Visually Challenged users. There are important tasks like getting a berth booked on Railways Reservation Website, paying taxes at Income tax website etc. which are complex in nature and have span about multiple web pages. Such task may not be conveniently performed by a visually challenged user using assistive technologies like screen readers. Besides, the assistive tools may not be installed on a public terminal. This makes a disadvantage for visually challenged users since the web based facility to utilize these public utilities is even more needed for them than their visually able counterparts. Such important public utilities should be universally accessible without the need to install any assistive tool on the computer used. In this context, we have provided two frameworks using which, owners of the public utility websites may directly speech enables their existing websites for more important functionalities at a minimum cost and effort required. The first framework, Speech-Enabler makes use of existing technologies like JavaScript and speech API, therefore provides robust and lightweight solution to the accessibility problem. The other framework, SICE Framework is based on VoiceXML and Voice-Over Internet Protocol (VOIP). It can be used for developing web based interactive voice applications without the need of telephony. Thus, complex web data can be conveniently handled using customized two way dialogue based access system in a controlled way. Similarly, we have taken some initiative in quantitative evaluation of assistive tools for blinds by formulating a hierarchical model. Identifying various Performance Attributes and Usage Metrics, we have established relationship among these to obtain the Overall Performance Index of the assistive tools.

4

1.7 ORGANIZATION OF THESIS

This thesis work addresses to some of the important issues related to web accessibility in context of visually challenged users. The research first aims to design develop and implement an improved yet affordable speech based web browser for visually challenged users. The second objective is to study the problems and issues of accessibility related to visually challenged users which are of more general nature and need global attention. Our emphasis on direct speech enabling public utility sites for their more important functionalities is one such issue which needs immediate attention of big public website owners.

The thesis is divided into three parts and eight chapters:

PART 1

(Introduction, Literature Survey, Problem Identification and Issues)

CHAPTER 1: INTRODUCTION

This chapter consists of Research Problem Statement, Research Objectives and Research Scope and refinement in the area chosen. The proposed solution is discussed.

CHAPTER 2: BACKGROUND WORK

This chapter explores the issues related to accessibility, usability and navigability. Keyboard based accessibility for visually challenged is discussed. Applicability of W3C Recommendations on Accessibility and challenges posed by Web 2.0 are also highlighted. A brief survey of existing tools for browsing by the visually challenged like Screen Readers, Transcoders, Web based Interactive Systems, IVR based interactive systems, TTS on web like WebAnyWhere etc. is made. Advantages and weaknesses of these systems along with their critical evaluation are given.

PART 2

(Problem Solutions, Approaches and Methodologies)

CHAPTER 3: WACTA, THE SPEECH BASED WEB BROWSER

This chapter describes the design, development, implementation and evaluation of an enhanced speech based web browser for visually challenged users. Architecture, working methodology and unique features of WACTA web browser are discussed.

CHAPTER 4: DIRECT SPEECH-ENABLING THE PUBLIC UTILITY WEBSITES

In this chapter, we have provided a frameworks using which, owners of the public utility websites may directly speech enables their existing websites for more important functionalities at a minimum cost and effort required. The framework, makes use of existing technologies like JavaScript and speech API, therefore provides robust and lightweight solution to the accessibility problem.

CHAPTER 5: VOICEXML /VOIP BASED CLIENT INTERFACE FOR INTERACTIVE BROWSING

In this chapter, a framework based on VoiceXML and Voice-Over Internet Protocol (VOIP) has been presented which can be used for developing web based interactive voice applications without the need of telephony.

CHAPTER 6: PERFORMANCE EVALUATION OF INTERNET ASSISTIVE TOOLS

This chapter discusses problems and issues involved in performance evaluation of assistive tools for visually challenged users. A hierarchical model for performance measure has been presented by us.

PART 3

(Results and Findings, Discussion, Conclusions and Directions for Future Research)

CHAPTER 7: RESULTS AND DISCUSSION

This chapter deals with the important results and findings of the research work along with the performance evaluation of the developed systems. The suitability of the frameworks is also evaluated on the basis of their applicability for different types of tasks.

CHAPTER 8: CONCLUSIONS AND FUTURE DIRECTIONS

This chapter summarizes the whole work, its impact in academia & Industry and also indicates the possible scopes for future work.

CHAPTER 2
BACKGROUND WORK

Speech is a convenient medium of interaction for visually challenged users. Internet accessibility is made possible for them by providing an alternative speech-based interface for human-computer interaction. Visually challenged users generally have no difficulty in using ordinary keyboards. Thus, command based user input using speech recognition is generally not required by the visually challenged users since its incorporation may adversely affect reliability and usability of the browsing system.

2.1 PROBLEMS AND ISSUES
2.1.1 Accessibility, Usability and Navigability

Accessibility, Usability and Navigability are the terms that creates lot confusion and are frequently encountered in related literature. Therefore, it is important to unambiguously define them before proceeding further. Each is a tripartite [5] as it relates the three aspects: Web Page(s), Assistive tool and Blind User. This fact is depicted in Figure 1. These properties are defined in Table 1 from the aspect of each player concerned.

Accessibility refers to the ability of a user, despite disabilities or impairments, to use a resource. For Internet-based applications, accessibility means that all users can perceive, understand, navigate, interact with, and contribute to the Web [6]. Visually challenged users most often use the Internet for sending E-mails, looking for some specific information like reservation inquiry or examination result inquiry, mailing, Web based learning, accessing news sites or for chat. They may also wish to make some transaction on internet like purchase of an item or e-ticket. But due to various reasons inherent to the web pages as well as tools used to access these pages, they are not able to perform these tasks independently. As a result, they may require performing uncomfortable travels. The concept of e-Learning is well perceived by the visually challenged since it helps them in overcoming the basic problems of commuting by bringing the class room to their home: thereby circumventing any bias that human instructors or fellow students might have. Audio-only e-Learning through Internet can be much helpful for them but realizing such a system has major challenges for describing visual elements like photographs, graphics, diagrams and charts.

The first role to ensure accessibility, usability and navigability in webpage(s) lies with Web Authors/Web Developers who are expected to follow the accessibility guidelines during website creation. Assistive tools can, most often function correctly if the webpage is compliant to the accessibility guideline. Unfortunately, this is not always the case since a large percentage of web pages have inaccessible contents. Thus, the role of assistive tools becomes important in terms of enhancing accessibility, usability and

7

navigability of the webpage(s) so that blind users may be able to access and use them. However, they are required to become proficient in using the assistive tool as well as to find out tricks and ways to use the web against all odds. Thus, they also have to play a role to efficiently use the assistive tool.

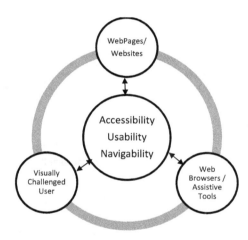

Fig. 2.1: The three aspects of Accessibility, Usability and Navigability

Property	Web Page(s)/ Web Author Perspective	Assistive Tools/Service Perspective	Blind User Perspective
Accessibility	The property of webpage(s) by virtue of which each element of it can be traversed by blind user using keyboard only.	The amount by which an assistive tool enhances the ability of a blind user to access each element of a web page using keyboard only.	The ability to access each element of a web page by blind user using keyboard only.
Usability	The property of webpage(s) by virtue of it a blind user can perform the tasks offered by webpage(s) independently.	The amount by which an assistive tool enhances the ability of a blind user to perform the tasks offered by webpage(s) independently.	The ability of a blind user to perform the tasks offered by webpage(s) independently
Navigability	The property of webpage(s) by virtue of it blind user can navigate around intra/ inter page links efficiently to access/ use its features.	The amount by which an assistive tool enhances the ability of a blind user to navigate around intra / inter page links efficiently to access/ use its features.	The ability of user to navigate around intra/ inter page links efficiently to access/ use its features.

Table 2.1: Accessibility, Usability and Navigability defined from the three perspectives

2.1.2 Keyboard based Accessibility

2.1.2.1 Windows Application Accessibility Vs Web Page Accessibility

The key difference between developing accessible desktop applications and developing accessible Web applications is that, while the Microsoft Win32 application program interface allows the writing of accessibility members on arbitrary controls, HTML is read-only for roles and events. A browser maps HTML tags to MSAA values, and the developer has no direct access to them.

It is strange that complete suite is available in Microsoft technologies for developing accessible desktop applications (Microsoft Active Accessibility/UI Automation) whereas there is no suite for web page accessibility. In the Operating System Windows 7, a narrator has been provided for Desktop Controls accessibility which does not work on web pages.

As far as the Web accessibility is concerned, a lot of literature is available on how to design or create accessible web contents but there is a lack of literature on know-how of Accessible Technologies for Web.

2.1.2.2 Keys used in accessibility by visually challenged

To browse web pages effectively, navigation keys are to be used by the visually challenged users. The navigation keys are: TAB, SHIFT+TAB, CTRL+TAB, CTRL+SHIFT+TAB, UPARROW, DOWNARROW, LEFTARROW and RIGHTARROW. Besides, PGUP, PGDOWN, HOME, CONTROL and ALT keys are also used to control the narration of the web page.

2.1.2.3 Key Shortcuts based accessibility

Blind users seldom use mouse since it requires coordination of eyes and position of hand. It is convenient for them to use keyboard shortcuts for inputting commands in GUI environment. Therefore, screen readers provide a set of keyboard shortcuts to use their various functionalities by visually challenged users. They require learning these key shortcut based commands to use the web effectively. Therefore, it is desirable that all the screen readers follow a standard notation for keyboard shortcut based commands meant for accessibility.

2.1.3 Role of Web Developers

Assistive Technologies (ATs) like screen readers make the use of underlying DOM (Document Object Model) structure to narrate the webpage elements to a visually challenged user. To ensure that ATs work correctly on a webpage, web developers must

10

follow the W3C and other guidelines while creating the websites. Unfortunately, due to lack of awareness among web developers, this requirement is not adequately met and as a result, a large amount of web content remains inaccessible to ATs and visually challenged users. An important checkpoint that a web developer should perform before launching of the website is to navigate through the links and form controls on a page using the keyboard only (for example, using the "Tab" key). Making sure that all links and form controls can be accessed without using the mouse, and that the links clearly indicate what they lead to. Overall Simplicity of the web page is a pre-requisite for ensuring the accessibility of a web page [7].

2.1.4 Role of Assistive Tools

Various assistive tools for using web by blind users have been designed using approaches like context based approach, semantic approach, annotation based approach, text summarization, etc. These assistive tools try to enhance the power of blind user by performing one or more of the following changes:

(A) Provide TTS (Text to speech) service i.e. speaking out the content of web page and giving speech feedback to user input by echoing the character typed. (Basic Service).
(B) Make the search informed using some heuristics, thereby reducing the time taken to search some information on web page.
(C) Providing better control over web page element by the means of shortcut keys,
(D) Take to some otherwise inaccessible content.
(E) Take to some otherwise unreachable link / form element
(F) Reduce the no of links (Performances) required to traverse to reach to some element on web page.
(G) Simplify the webpage both in structure and content.
(H) Providing a better understanding of web page layout / structure.
(I) Providing a better understanding of images by the means of reading out their ALT text.
(J) Providing a better understanding of visual diagrams by interpreting them.

2.1.5 Role of Visually Challenged Users

Screen readers are sophisticated programs with considerable functionality – an expert user, whether sighted or blind, is needed to use these programs effectively. As compare to visual User Interfaces, that are self explanatory to the sighted users, screen readers may use several keyboard shortcuts to access the web effectively. The usage of these shortcuts is to be learnt by visually challenged users. There may be several modes in which visually challenged user may use screen reader depending on the need for access. Each mode may be activated by a keyboard shortcut to be pressed by user. Thus, proper training and learning of visually challenged users is also a key to effective use of assistive technology.

11

2.1.6 Various strategies to design the Web Accessibility tools

Several strategies are used to address the issues related to speech based web access for blind users. The first strategy employs a client based assistive tool (e.g. screen reader) to speak out the web content in some desired order. Generally, such tools are required to be installed locally on user computer. Second strategy makes the use of a proxy server or client based transcoder [8] that renders the web content after converting it to a more accessible form. Another strategy used is to speech enable a website directly by the web author thus requiring no assistive tool on part of blind user. None of these strategies provide perfect solution for the problem and each may have its own merit and drawback. Usability of the screen readers is mainly constrained by the complex structure/ poor accessibility of web pages. The transcoder based access services may not be applied for secure sites as they do not permit to access or modify its code by a third party. Direct Speech enabling a site may be difficult to maintain.

2.1.7 Universal Vs. Local Installation

An assistive tool may require to be locally installed on user machine or it may be provided online as a web service. The first approach constraints the use of the assistive tool by its availability in installed form whereas in the second approach local installation is not required. Thus, user can access the web using any public terminal.

2.2 W3C RECOMMENDATIONS ON ACCESSIBILITY

The concrete definition of Web accessibility is established by the Web accessibility standards. The most significant Web accessibility standards are developed and published by the same organization that standardizes the pivotal Web technologies in the first place; the World Wide Web Consortium. In addition to the education and outreach value for the community, this ensures that accessibility features are considered in the standardization process of the core Web technologies.

2.2.1 W3C and WAI

The World Wide Web Consortium (W3C) is an international community that develops standards to ensure the long-term growth of the Web. The W3C mission is to lead the Web to its full potential. Currently, the main W3C activities include Web design and applications, Web architecture, Semantic Web, Extensible Markup Language (XML) technologies, Web of services, Web of devices, and browsers and authoring tools. The W3C vision is the One Web; the Web for all and the Web on everything.

Besides technologies, W3C develops also guidelines for their usage. Following the Web development and the interests of its membership, the W3C is also continuously exploring new prominent areas for Web standardization, e.g. in the form of joint events and W3Cworkshops.

In 1997, W3C launched the Web Accessibility Initiative (WAI) that falls into the Web design and applications domain. In brief, WAI works with organizations around the world to develop strategies, guidelines, and resources to help make the Web accessible to people with disabilities. WAI activities follow the W3C Process which explains the rigorous standardization process in detail World Wide Web Consortium Process Document [9].

2.2.2 WAI Specifications

To date, the WAI has published standard guidelines and specifications related to the following aspects of Web accessibility:

1. Web Content Accessibility Guidelines (WCAG)
2. Authoring Tool Accessibility Guidelines (ATAG)
3. User Agent Accessibility Guidelines (UAAG)
4. Evaluation and Report Language (EARL)
5. Accessible Rich Internet Applications (WAI-ARIA)

These consider representing Web content (e.g. HTML pages), authoring tools (e.g. functions supporting accessibility evaluation during authoring), the user agent aspect (e.g. ability to use keyboard for input and to pause dynamic content), publishing evaluation reports (e.g. reporting suggestions how to improve the accessibility of a certain application), and dynamic Web content (e.g. scripting).

Besides the standard guidelines, WAI produces also other significant accessibility resources. In particular, abstract guidelines and technique-specific or explanatory considerations are presented in separate specifications, complemented with informative resources.

2.2.3 Web Content Accessibility

Perhaps the most significant Web Accessibility standard is established by the Web Content Accessibility Guidelines (WCAG) [10]. The current stable version, published in 2008, is the WCAG 2.0.

WCAG 2.0 standard considers the accessibility of Web content. The content accessibility guidelines specification is organized around four abstract principles: Accessible Web content is perceivable, operable, understandable, and robust. Each

13

principle is explained with one or more intuitively understandable design goals, asserted as guidelines.

WCAG 2.0 asserts total 12 guidelines:

1. Perceivable
    1. Provide text alternatives for any non-text content so that it can be changed into other forms people need, such as large print, braille, speech, symbols or simpler language.
    2. Provide alternatives for time-based media.
    3. Create content that can be presented in different ways (for example simpler layout) without losing information or structure.
    4. Make it easier for users to see and hear content including separating foreground from background.
2. Operable
    1. Make all functionality available from a keyboard.
    2. Provide users enough time to read and use content.
    3. Do not design content in a way that is known to cause seizures.
    4. Provide ways to help users navigate, find content, and determine where they are.
3. Understandable
    1. Make text content readable and understandable.
    2. Make Web pages appear and operate in predictable ways.
    3. Help users avoid and correct mistakes.
4. Robust
    1. Maximize compatibility with current and future user agents, including assistive technologies.

For purposes of conformance evaluation, each guideline is associated success criteria. Three levels of conformance are defined: A (lowest), AA, and AAA (highest or "best"). These are designed to meet the needs of different accessibility use cases.

The WCAG 2.0 is also associated with a variety of sufficient and advisory techniques. These explain how to meet the success criteria and beyond, using a specific technology, such as hypertext, scripting, or style sheet content.

When compared to the intuitive notion of accessibility, the main limitation of the WCAG 2.0 is the relatively modest support for evaluating cognitive accessibility. Thus, while the guidelines and the success criteria highlight good things such as the importance of intuitive structures, avoiding unusual words, and the clarity of overall presentation, there is still a need for introducing additional, domain-specific understandability criteria. This is because the WCAG 2.0 considers understandability from a global perspective, without making references to a particular application domain, assumed education, or specific user attributes.

In practice, the WCAG standard provides a normative definition and an evaluation system for accessible Web content: A Web application is accessible if it meets the success criteria for the WCAG 2.0 guidelines (at least) on the level A of conformance.

2.2.4 Authoring Tool Accessibility

The Authoring Tool Accessibility Guidelines (ATAG) provides guidelines for software and services that people use to produce Web pages and other Web content. The currently stable version of the Authoring Tool Accessibility Guidelines is the ATAG 1.0, published in 2000.

The purpose of ATAG 1.0 is twofold: to assist developers in designing authoring tools that produce accessible Web content and to assist developers in creating an accessible authoring interface. In particular, since many Web applications include authoring interfaces, the scope of ATAG is much wider than simply the commercial off-the-shelf Web authoring tools. For instance, consider a Web application that keeps a record of registered users and provides them an authoring interface for managing their contact information.

ATAG 1.0 introduces seven guidelines, associated with checkpoints of three priorities and three conformance levels: A (lowest), AA, and AAA (highest). In brief, ATAG 1.0 aims authoring Web content that is accessible with respect to the WCAG (1.0) specification. As a consequence, some ATAG checkpoints have multiple priorities, capturing the relationship with the WCAG (1.0) conformance levels.

The current ATAG 1.0 guidelines are as follows [11]:

1. Support accessible authoring practices.
2. Generate standard markup.
3. Support the creation of accessible content.
4. Provide ways of checking and correcting inaccessible content.
5. Integrate accessibility solutions into the overall "look and feel".
6. Promote accessibility in help and documentation.
7. Ensure that the authoring tool is accessible to authors with disabilities.

It is worth noticing that ATAG requires that the authoring tools and its documentation are themselves accessible. This is significant since it people experiencing accessibility problems are more likely to be interested in authoring accessible content.

The forthcoming version, ATAG 2.0 will probably change the wording and the organization of the guidelines somewhat. In particular, ATAG 2.0 is expected to reflect the abstract principles and the structure of WCAG 2.0.

2.2.5 User Agent Accessibility

The User Agent Accessibility Guidelines (UAAG) considers the accessibility of the Web user agent, in particularly with respect to Web content accessibility. In this context, user agents include Web browsers, media players, and assistive technologies.

The purpose of the UAAG 1.0 is to provide guidelines for designing accessible Web user agents. As a consequence, the audience of UAAG is much smaller than of WCAG or ATAG. In brief, the UAAG points out the user agent implementation principles for interacting with accessible content, with a special requirement of being able to communicate with other software, especially assistive technologies.

UAAG 1.0 introduces 12 guidelines, associated with checkpoints of three priorities and three conformance levels: A (lowest), AA, and AAA (highest). Informative resources about different techniques are also available. Unlike the other guidelines, UAAG also briefly considers challenges such as accessible installation and user control over their environment when accessing the Web. In addition, the UAAG 1.0 defines a system called conformance profile labels. This supports developing and documenting (specialized) user agents that conform only to a subset of all conceivable accessibility features.

The UAAG 1.0 guidelines are as follows [12]:

1. Support input and output device-independence.
2. Ensure user access to all content.
3. Allow configuration not to render some content that may reduce accessibility.
4. Ensure user control of rendering.
5. Ensure user control of user interface behavior.
6. Implement interoperable application programming interfaces.
7. Observe operating environment conventions.
8. Implement specifications that benefit accessibility.
9. Provide navigation mechanisms.
10. Orient the user.
11. Allow configuration and customization.
12. Provide accessible user agent documentation and help.

The forthcoming UAAG 2.0 will probably change the wording and the organization of the guidelines a bit. Again, UAAG 2.0 is expected to reflect the abstract principles and structure of WCAG 2.0 and the related documents.

2.2.6   Accessible Rich Internet Applications Suite

The Accessible Rich Internet Applications Suite (WAI-ARIA) defines a way to make dynamic content and advanced user interface controls accessible to people, regardless of disability. This includes content developed with Ajax, HTML, JavaScript, and related technologies [13].

The basic idea of WAI-ARIA is that complex web applications become inaccessible when assistive technologies cannot determine the semantics behind portions of a document. Accessibility problems may also arise when the user is unable to effectively navigate to all parts of documents in a usable way.

2.2.7   Challenges posed by Web 2.0

Web 2.0 is characterized by rich visual contents, user centric in form and contents. User, who was earlier at receiving end, has become the content provider and web-author. The role of site owner has been reduced to merely managerial and business logic provider. This development has posed a lot of challenges to assistive technology. End users while authoring the web may not follow the accessibility guidelines due to unawareness. Thus, certain contents provided by them may not be accessible to the assistive technology. Second, dynamic features of web 2.0 prevent screen readers to correctly access the web content. The content narrated by the screen reader may completely change during narration and prevent the screen reader to correctly render the contents to the user. Rich contents like embedded Image/ button links and anchors remain inaccessible to the screen readers.

2.3   EXISTING SYSTEMS

Various systems have been developed using approaches like content analysis, document reading rules, context summary, summary/gist based, semantic analysis, sequential information flow in web pages etc. But these systems have a number of issues which make them less usable. First, they are essentially screen readers or their extension. Second, they provide only browsing and do not support other applications like mail, form-filling, transaction, chat etc. A brief survey of some important existing browsing systems has been made in this section.

Some of the most popular screen-readers are JAWS [14] and IBM's Home Page Reader [15]. JAWS is a popular state-of-art screen reader developed by Freedom Scientific. JAW 13.7 is the current stable version which supports Windows 7 Operating System. Besides sequential access of web content, it has rich set of key shortcuts that can be used by visually impaired users to access the web.

"Emacspeak" [16] is a free screen reader for Emacs developed by T. V. Raman and first released in May 1995; it is tightly integrated with Emacs, allowing it to render intelligible and useful content rather than parsing the graphics.

Brookes Talk [17] is a web browser developed in Oxford Brookes University in 90's. Brookes Talk provides function keys for accessing the web page. Brookes Talk reads out the webpage using speech synthesis in words, sentences and paragraph mode by parsing the web page content. It also uses some mechanism for searching the suitable results using search engines and supports a conceptual model of website too. It supports modeling of information on web page and summarizes the web page content.

Csurf [18] is developed by Stony Brook University. Csurf is context based browsing system. Csurf brings together content analysis, natural language processing and machine learning algorithm to help visually disabled to quickly identify relevant information. Csurf is composed of interface manager, context analyzer, browser object from tress processor and dialog generator. Csurf web browser uses the functionality of voice XML, JSAPI, freeTTS, Sphinx, JREXAPI, etc.

Aster (Audio system for technical reading)[19], developed by T. V. Raman, permits visually disabled individuals to manually define their own document reading rules. Aster is implemented by using Emacs as a main component for reading. It recognizes the markup language as logical structure of web page internally. Then user can either listen to entire document or any part of it.

Some researchers have also proposed to extract the web content using semantics [20].

Hearsay [21] is developed at Stony Brook University. It is a multimodal dialog system in which browser reads the webpage under the control of the user. It analyzes the web page content like HTML, DOM tree, segments web page and on the basis of this generates VoiceXML dialogues.

A Vernacular Speech Interface for People with visual Impairment named "Shruti" has been developed at Media Lab Asia research hub at IIT Kharagpur, India. It is an embedded Indian language Text-to-Speech system that accepts text inputs in two Indian languages - Hindi and Bengali, and produces near natural speech output.

Shruti-Drishti, [22] is a Computer Aided Text-to-Speech and Text-to-Braille System developed in collaboration with CDAC Pune and Webel Mediatronics Ltd, (WML) Kolkata. This is an integrated Text-to-Speech and Text-to-Braille system which enables persons with visual impairment to access the electronic documents from the conference websites in speech and Braille form.

Screen reading software SAFA (Screen Access For All) [23] has been developed by Media Lab Asia research hub at IIT Kharagpur in collaboration with National Association for the Blind, New Delhi in Vernacular language to enable the visually disabled persons to use PC. This enables a person with visual impairment to operate PC using speech output. It gives speech output support for windows environment and for both English and Hindi scripts.

As far as general surfing is concerned, above mentioned screen readers are important and useful tool to the visually disabled. But, in case of complex tasks like information query, complex navigation, form-filling or some transaction, they do not work to the level of satisfaction. Screen Readers provide accessibility through abundant use of shortcut keys for which visually disabled have to be trained. Also, the screen readers need to be purchased and installed on the local machine which prevents them to use the internet on any public terminal.

Despite their shortcomings, Screen Readers have been the primary tool for using internet by visually challenged. Unfortunately, most of the popular and workable screen readers are proprietary and bear a heavy price tag. For example, cost of JAWS, a popular screen reader by Freedom Scientific for single user license is around $900. This cost is 10 times higher than that of Windows7 operating system! The cost is evidently too high to be afforded by an average Indian individual with visual disability. High cost is also attributed by small product market for assistive tools. There are ATs in freeware domain but they are not popular since most of them may not provide adequate functionalities.

2.4 TEXT TO SPEECH (TTS) ON WEB

Prospects of TTS on web are gaining momentum gradually. At present, fetching mp3 on a remote web service is the only standard way for converting text to speech. APIs used for this purpose are proprietary and provide text to speech services, e.g. BrowseAloud [24] is a TTS service using which a web site can be speech enabled. Google Translate Service also has a TTS feature. Although many websites have provision of reading its contents, but it is limited to playing the content as a single mp3 file. There is no provision for interactive navigation and form filling in most of them. Implementation of TTS as a browser extension would go in a big way to simplify the text to speech related issues in future.

WebAnywhere [25] is an open source online TTS developed at Washington University for surfing the web. It requires no special software to be installed on the client machine and, therefore, enables visually disabled people to access the web from any computer. It can also be used as a tool to test the accessibility of a website under construction. WebAnywhere generates speech remotely and uses pre-fetching strategies designed to reduce perceived latency. It also uses a server side transformational proxy

19

that makes web pages appear to come from local server to overcome cross-site scripting restrictions. On the client side, Javascript is used to support user interaction by deciding which sound to be played by the sound player.

Like screen readers, WebAnyWhere reads out the elements in sequential order by default. Although few shortcut keys are assigned to control the page elements, user has to make an assessment of the whole page in order to proceed further. In websites with poor accessibility design, user may be trapped during a complex navigation.

Although WebAnyWhere is a step forward in the direction of online installation-free accessibility, it has certain limitations: As the contents in WebAnyWhere are received through a third party, they may not be treated reliable. Fear of malware attacks, phishing etc. is associated with such access. Secure sites cannot be accessed using this approach as they do not allow manipulating their contents. This is a major drawback since most of the important tasks like bank transaction, filling examination forms, using e-mail services etc. are performed over secure sites. These drawbacks compromise the usability of WebAnyWhere and limit it to an information access tool only.

CHAPTER 3
WACTA, THE SPEECH BASED WEB BROWSER

3.1   INTRODUCTION

In confirmation to the "Research by Application Development" philosophy adopted and as a part of this research work, an enhanced speech based web browser named 'WACTA' has been designed and developed with a vision of providing an improved yet affordable and easy to use web browser for visually challenged users. The system has been implemented for Microsoft Windows 7 Operating System in programming language C# and .NET framework 4.0. Microsoft Speech API (SAPI 5.0) has been used for narration of the text and input feedback.

WACTA web Browser has several unique features that distinct it from other screen readers. First, the speech based web browser has been implemented completely using managed code. So far, web browsers have been implemented using unmanaged code. Implementation in managed code offers better reliability as automatic garbage collection is possible in managed code only. Second, speech features have been integrated in the WACTA browser itself. It can be used in many modes depending upon the user need and user disability level. Thus, there are auto sequential, manual sequential, newsreader mode, interactive mode, analytical mode and mouse Glimpse mode (for partially blind user) which can be chosen from among menu or using the key shortcuts. At any time, visually challenged user can make switch over from one mode to another. It aids to minimizing the time required to complete a given task.

3.2   SYSTEM DESIGN

This section describes the design issues, conceptual architecture, and interactions among various sub components of the proposed system.

3.2.1 Conceptual Architecture

Fig. 3.1 describes the conceptual architecture of the WACTA web browser. The system is based on narration of the webpage in a controlled way as well speech feedback for user input. The requested web page is loaded on the browser. The web page is parsed to obtain its constituent elements. It is then sent to the Text to Speech (TTS) to generate the speech equivalent of the desired text. User Input is given by keyboard input on the web browser address bar. A speech based feedback is generated for each key press thereby assuring the user of correct key press. Various modes of access have been provided to control the web content in a desired way.

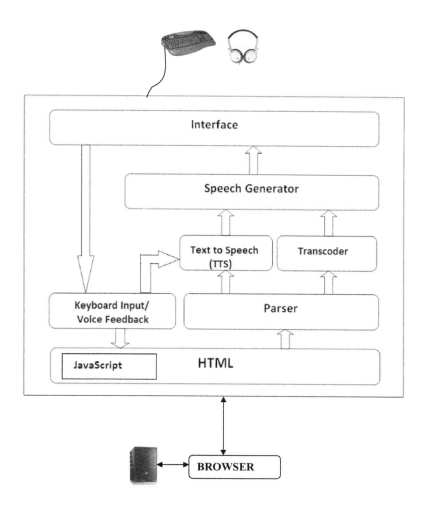

Fig 3.1: Schematic diagram of the WACTA Web Browser

22

The proposed System has the following modes of working:

3.2.2   Link Navigation Mode

In this mode, user can navigate among links to quickly reach to the webpage to get desired information. Link navigation mode can help understanding the map of the website. Thus, s/he can access the basic structure of the website.

3.2.3   Navigate All Mode

In the second mode, each element of the web page is traversed by the user in a controlled manner. This mode provides better control for moving around the web page and is helpful in form filling, making queries etc.

3.2.4   Newsreader Mode

This mode may be useful for news reading, gathering knowledge on some topic, e-learning etc. In newsreader mode, the contents of the webpage are narrated automatically by the browser.

3.2.5   Page Analytics Mode

In this mode, web page details e.g. web site domain name, details of links, images, forms etc. is narrated in the desired way.

3.2.6   Query Mode

In this mode, user can locate the desired information within the website by inputting a keyword in the textbox.

3.2.7   Text Glimpse through mouse Mode

In this mode, the browser speaks out glimpses of the portion on which mouse is right clicked by the user. Visually challenged users rely on keyboard to perform user inputs; therefore mouse is not normally useful to them. However, this mode is primarily suitable for users with low vision who may not read the content of the text visible to them. Thus, s(he) can directly go to the portion of their interest on the web page using mouse click after listening the underlying text.

3.2.8   Switch over among modes

Switch over to any of the available modes can be made by using designated key shortcut at any time. Thus, a visually challenged user may make the combination of the modes to perform navigation around the webpage in a more controlled way.

3.2.9 Key Shortcuts

Besides the above stated three modes, several key shortcuts identical to those available with the screen reader JAWS are also provided. Key Shortcuts are a convenient and preferred mode of working by visually challenged users. Only problem is they are to be learnt and remembered. The usage proficiency is increased with their frequent use. Some of the important functionalities for which key shortcuts have been provided are: go to the next form element, Go to the next heading; Go to the top of next column, Go to Begin of the page, Go to the Address Bar etc.

3.2.10 Informed Search

Using various available modes and features intuitively, visually challenged user may access his/ her text of interest very quickly. Thus, rather than making blind sequential depth first search, the WACTA user makes use of informed search to locate the information on the webpage.

Fig. 3.2 depicts the Use Case diagram for WACTA Web Browser. The six modes of usage makes the complete system using which a visually challenged user can perform an informed search to get the content of his/ her interest. At any time, user can make switch over to another mode using the assigned key shortcut for that mode. Thus, visually challenged user can make intelligent guesses to access the relevant content with the help of available modes. Mouse Glimpse mode may be used by partially visually challenged users to listen a portion of web page they find difficult to read normally.

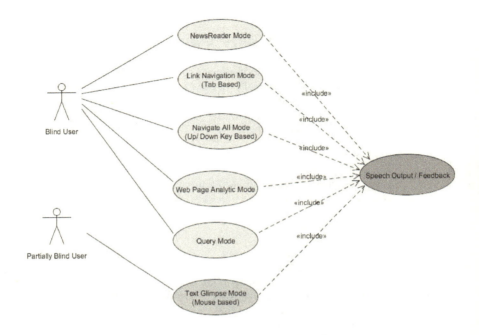

Fig. 3.2: Use-Case Diagram of WACTA Web Browser

3.3 SYSTEM DEVELOPMENT AND IMPLEMENTATION

The following subsections describe the implementation details of speech based web browser WACTA for visually challenged users.

3.3.1 Platform and Language

Microsoft Windows 7 has been the chosen operating system for the implementation due to its popularity and wide acceptance. Further, due to flexibility provided by it in the development of applications, .Net platform with C# language has been used for development of the prototype Framework. Microsoft Language Interface provides better interface in term of functionality and processing power.

3.3.2 .NET Framework

Microsoft .NET is software that connects information, people, System and devices. It spans clients, servers, and developer tools. It consists of all kinds of software, including web based applications, smart client applications and XML web services. It also contains components to facilitate integration and of sharing of data and functionality over a network through standard, platform independent protocols such as XML, SOAP and HTTP. Developer tools such as Microsoft Visual Studio.NET 2008 provide an integrated development environment for maximizing developer productivity with .NET framework.

3.3.3 The WebBrowser Class

To create the skeleton of the speech based web browser WACTA, the WebBrowser class (Namespace: System.Windows.Forms) has been used. The WebBrowser class offers rich features and functionalities that can be used to control the output of various web page elements in the desired order.

Table 3.1 summarizes the attributes, methods, and events of WebBrowser Class used in the WACTA Web Browsing System.

Property Name	Description
CanGoForward	Gets a value indicating whether a subsequent page in navigation history is available, which allows theGoForward method to succeed.
CanGoBack	Gets a value indicating whether a previous page in navigation history is available, which allows the GoBackmethod to succeed.
Document	Gets an HtmlDocument representing the Web page currently displayed in the WebBrowser control.
DocumentStream	Gets or sets a stream containing the contents of the Web page displayed in the WebBrowser control.
DocumentText	Gets or sets the HTML contents of the page displayed in the WebBrowser control.
DocumentTitle	Gets the title of the document currently displayed in the WebBrowser control.
DocumentType	Gets the type of the document currently displayed in the WebBrowser control.

Table 3.1(i): Properties of WebBrowser Class

26

Method Name	Description
Focus	Sets input focus to the control. (Inherited from Control.)
GetChildAtPoint(Point)	Retrieves the child control that is located at the specified coordinates. (Inherited from Control.)
Navigate(String)	Loads the document at the specified Uniform Resource Locator (URL) into the WebBrowser control, replacing the previous document.
Navigate(Uri)	Loads the document at the location indicated by the specified Uri into the WebBrowser control, replacing the previous document
Navigate(Uri, Boolean)	Loads the document at the location indicated by the specified Uri into a new browser window or into the WebBrowser control.
Stop	Cancels any pending navigation and stops any dynamic page elements, such as background sounds and animations.

Table 3.1(ii): Methods of WebBrowser Class

Event Name	Description
DocumentCompleted	Occurs when the WebBrowser control finishes loading a document.
DocumentTitleChanged	Occurs when the DocumentTitle property value changes.
Navigating	Occurs before the WebBrowser control navigates to a new document.
Navigated	Occurs when the WebBrowser control has navigated to a new document and has begun loading it.
PreviewKeyDown	Occurs before the KeyDown event when a key is pressed while focus is on this control. (Inherited fromControl.)

Table 3.1(iii): Events of WebBrowser class used

3.3.4 Web Page Analytics

To get the access to various elements of a web page, its DOM structure is explored. Document Object Model (DOM) is an Application Programming Interface (API) for valid HTML and well formed XML documents. It is based on an object structure that closely resembles the structure of the documents it models. It allows applications to dynamically access content, structure and style of the documents. DOM is not restricted to a specific platform or programming language. Figure 3.3 represents the DOM structure for a web page.

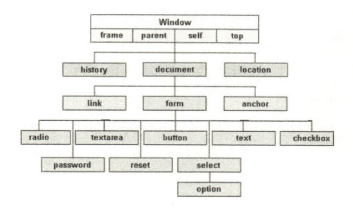

Fig. 3.3: DOM Structure of a Web Page

Following classes have been used in extracting the HTML elements from web pages:

3.3.5 HtmlDocument class

This class provides top level programmatic access to an HTML document hosted by the WebBrowser Control. It belongs to System. Windows.Forms namespace. Properties, methods and Events of this class used in the implementation of WACTA are described in Table 3.2(i), (ii) and (iii) respectively. When the document has focus, but no element of the document has been given focus, ActiveElement returns the element corresponding to the <BODY> tag. If the document does not have focus, ActiveElement returns null.

28

Property Name	Description
ActiveElement	Provides the HtmlElement which currently has user input focus.
All	Gets an instance of HtmlElementCollection, which stores all HtmlElement objects for the document.
Body	Gets the HtmlElement for the BODY tag.
Focused	Gets a value indicating whether the document has user input focus.
Forms	Gets a collection of all of the <FORM> elements in the document.
Links	Gets a list of all the hyperlinks within this HTML document.
Title	Gets or sets the text value of the <TITLE> tag in the current HTML document.
Url	Gets the URL describing the location of this document.

Table 3.2(i): Properties of HtmlDocument class used

Method Name	Description
Focus	Sets user input focus on the current document
GetElementFromPoint	Retrieves the HTML element located at the specified client coordinates.
GetElementsByTagName	Retrieve a collection of elements with the specified tag.

Table 3.2(ii): Methods of HtmlDocument class used

Event Name	Description
Click	Occurs when the user clicks anywhere on the document.
ContextMenuShowing	Occurs when the user requests to display the document's context menu.
Focusing	Occurs before focus is given to the document.
LosingFocus	Occurs while focus is leaving a control.
MouseDown	Occurs when the user clicks the left mouse button.
MouseOver	Occurs when the mouse is moved over the document.
MouseUp	Occurs when the user releases the left mouse button.
Stop	Occurs when navigation to another Web page is halted.

Table 3.2(iii): Events of HtmlDocument class used

29

3.3.6 HtmlElement Class

HtmlElement class represents an HTML element inside of a web page. It belongs to System.Windows.Forms namespace. Properties, methods and Events of this class used in the implementation of WACTA are described in Table 3.3(i), (ii) and (iii) respectively.

Property Name	Description
All	Gets an HtmlElementCollection of all elements underneath the current element.
CanHaveChildren	Gets a value indicating whether this element can have child elements.
Children	Gets an HtmlElementCollection of all children of the current element.
Document	Gets the HtmlDocument to which this element belongs.
Enabled	Gets or sets whether the user can input data into this element.
FirstChild	Gets the next element below this element in the document tree.
InnerHtml	Gets or sets the HTML markup underneath this element.
InnerText	Gets or sets the text assigned to the element.
Name	Gets or sets the name of the element.
NextSibling	Gets the next element at the same level as this element in the document tree.
OuterHtml	Gets or sets the current element's HTML code.
OuterText	Gets or sets the current element's text.
Parent	Gets the current element's parent element.
TabIndex	Gets or sets the location of this element in the tab order.
TagName	Gets the name of the HTML tag.

Table 3.3(i): Properties of HtmlElement class used

Method Name	Description
Focus	Puts user input focus on the current element.
GetAttribute	Retrieves the value of the named attribute on the element.
GetElementsByTagName	Retrieves a collection of elements represented in HTML by the specified HTML tag.
GetType	Gets the Type of the current instance.
ToString	Returns a string that represents the current object.

Table 3.3(ii): Methods of HtmlElement class used

Event Name	Description
Focusing	Occurs when the element first receives user input focus.
GotFocus	Occurs when the element has received user input focus.
KeyDown	Occurs when the user presses a key on the keyboard.
KeyPress	Occurs when the user presses and releases a key on the keyboard.
KeyUp	Occurs when the user releases a key on the keyboard.
LosingFocus	Occurs when the element is losing user input focus
LostFocus	Occurs when the element has lost user input focus.

Table 3.3(iii): Events of HtmlElement class used

3.3.7 HtmlElementCollection class

HtmlElementCollection class Defines a collection of HtmlElement objects.

Properties of this class used in the implementation of *WACTA are* described in Table 3.4.

Property Name	Description
Count	Gets the number of elements in the collection.
Item[Int32]	Gets an item from the collection by specifying its numerical index.
Item[String]	Gets an item from the collection by specifying its name.

Table 3.4: Properties of HtmlElementCollection class used

3.3.8 SpeechSynthesizer Class

SpeechSynthesizer class of .NET Framework has been used to speech enable the webpage using the WACTA web browser. The class belongs to System.Speech.Synthesis Namespace. SpeechSynthesizer class Provides access to the functionality of the installed a speech synthesis engine, i.e. Microsoft Speech API 5.0 (SAPI).

To ensure the consistency in speech output/ feedback in various modes of working, only single instance of SpeechSynthesizer class has been created and used throughout the application. This approach prevents the running of multiple narrator instances simultaneously. Properties, methods and Events of this class used in the implementation of WACTA are described in Table 3.5 (i), (ii) and (iii) respectively.

Property Name	Description
Rate	Gets or sets the speaking rate of the SpeechSynthesizer object.
State	Gets the speaking state of the SpeechSynthesizer object.
Voice	Gets information about the current voice of the SpeechSynthesizer object.
Volume	Get or sets the output volume of the SpeechSynthesizer object.

Table 3.5(i): Properties of SpeechSynthesizer class used

Event Name	Description
SpeakCompleted	Raised when the SpeechSynthesizer completes the speaking of a prompt.
SpeakProgress	Raised after the SpeechSynthesizer speaks each individual word of a prompt.
SpeakStarted	Raised when the SpeechSynthesizer begins the speaking of a prompt.
StateChanged	Raised when the state of the SpeechSynthesizer changes.

Table 3.5 (ii): Events of SpeechSynthesizer class used

Method Name	Description
Dispose	Disposes the SpeechSynthesizer object and releases resources used during the session.
GetInstalledVoices()	Returns all of the installed speech synthesis (text-to-speech) voices.
Pause	Pauses the speaking of a prompt by a SpeechSynthesizer object.
Resume	Resumes the speaking of a prompt by the SpeechSynthesizer object after it has been paused.
SelectVoice	Selects a specific voice by name.
SelectVoiceByHints(VoiceGender)	Selects a voice with a specific gender.
SetOutputToNull	Configures the SpeechSynthesizer object to not send output from synthesis operations to a device, file, or stream.
Speak(Prompt)	Synchronously speaks the contents of a Prompt object.
Speak(PromptBuilder)	Synchronously speaks the contents of a PromptBuilder object.
Speak(String)	Synchronously speaks the contents of a string.
SpeakAsync(Prompt)	Asynchronously speaks the contents of a Prompt object.
SpeakAsync(PromptBuilder)	Asynchronously speaks the contents of a PromptBuilder object.
SpeakAsync(String)	Asynchronously speaks the contents of a string.
SpeakAsyncCancel	Cancels the asynchronous synthesis operation for a queued prompt.
SpeakAsyncCancelAll	Cancels all queued, asynchronous, speech synthesis operations.
ToString	Returns a string that represents the current object.

Table 3.5(iii): Methods of SpeechSynthesizer class used

3.3.9 Newsreader style Navigation

This module reads out the text as displayed on the web page in Newsreader style. The mode does not inform or permit to interact with UI elements on the webpage. At any instance of time, the narration can be pause by pressing CONTROL key. The narration can be discarded altogether by pressing ESC key.

The module is implemented using the InnerText property of the HtmlElement class. InnerText property of the html element for Body tag of the Web page returns the complete text content of the web page in sequential order. Table 3.6 shows the code snippet for it.

```
private void buttonNews_Click(object sender, EventArgs e)
    {

        HtmlElement el = webBrowser1.Document.Body;
        el.Focus();
        HtmlElement el1;
        el1 = webBrowser1.Document.ActiveElement;
        if (el1 != null && el1.InnerText != null)
        {

            syn.SpeakAsync((el1.InnerText).ToString());

        }


    }
```

Table 3.6: Newsreader Style Navigation

3.3.10 Tab based Navigation

The Tab key is the primary mechanism for navigating of a web page by visually challenged user. The Tab key visits only those controls with a tab stop. Tab Key based navigation allows to traverse through all the focusable User Interface (UI) elements. These elements have their tabIndex property set to a positive integer value. Tab based traversal allows user to visit the focusable elements in the increasing order of the tabIndex value of the elements. Normally, Html Links, Anchors and Form elements are assigned tabIndex value to enable them to get focus. However, any html element can be enabled by the web designer to get focus. Tab based navigation is useful for tasks like form filling, choosing a website from search results etc.

The code for Tab key based navigation has been implemented in the handler for 'Focusing' event of HtmlElement currently getting user input focus i.e.,

ActiveElement. The Focusing event is registered in the DocumentCompleted method of the WebBrowser class. This can be viewed in the code snippet in the Table 3.7.

```
webBrowser1.Document.ActiveElement.Focusing += new
HtmlElementEventHandler(ActiveElement_Focusing);
```

```
void ActiveElement_Focusing(object sender, HtmlElementEventArgs e)
    {
        HtmlElement el = webBrowser1.Document.ActiveElement;
        if (webBrowser1.Document != null && el.TagName != "<BODY>" &&
webBrowser1.Document.ActiveElement != null)
        {
            HtmlElement elem = webBrowser1.Document.ActiveElement;

            syn.SpeakAsync(elem.TagName.ToString());

            if (elem.TagName == "INPUT" || elem.TagName == "SELECT" ||
elem.TagName == "OPTION")
                syn.SpeakAsync(elem.GetAttribute("title"));

            if (elem.InnerText != null)
            {
                syn.SpeakAsync(elem.InnerText.ToString());
            }
        }

    }
```

Table 3.7: Tab based Navigation

3.3.11 Up/Down key based Navigation

Up / down key based traversal allows user to visit each HTML elements of the webpage in forward / backward order of their creation. This mode has been implemented in the event handler of PreviewKeyDown event of the WebBrowser class. Registering of this event is made in the DocumentCompleted method as shown in Table 3.8(a). The handler stores each element underneath the BODY Tag in the object of HtmlElementCollection type. Problems encountered in this implementation is that InnerText method of HtmlElement object returns the text which includes the text of all the children nodes. Thus, it is required to separate the text of the current node only so that it can be spoken out. This issue has been resolved by selecting only those children of HtmlElementCollection that have a single child. Still, some elements may not be covered using this method for which string processing is used. This code is listed in the Table 3.8.

```
webBrowser1.PreviewKeyDown += new
PreviewKeyDownEventHandler(webBrowser1_PreviewKeyDown);

void webBrowser1_PreviewKeyDown(object sender, PreviewKeyDownEventArgs e)
        {
            HtmlElement el = webBrowser1.Document.Body;
            HtmlElementCollection htmCollect = el.All;
            int count = htmCollect.Count;
            //Down Key Press
            if (e.KeyCode == Keys.Down)
            {
                HtmlElement x = htmCollect[i];

                while (x.InnerText == null && i < count - 1)
                {
                    ++i;
                    x = htmCollect[i];
                }
                String str = x.InnerText;
                String str1 = x.InnerHtml;
                String str2;
                if (!x.CanHaveChildren && x.InnerText != null)
                    syn.SpeakAsync(x.InnerText);
                else if (x.CanHaveChildren && x.InnerText != null && x.InnerHtml
!= null)
                {
                    int j = 0;
                    while (j < str.Length && str[j] == str1[j])
                    {
                        j++;
                    }
                    str2 = str.Substring(0, j);
                    if (str2 != null)
                        syn.SpeakAsync(str2);
                }

                if (i < count - 1)
                    i++;
                else
                    i = 0;
            }

}
```

Table 3.8: Up/Down key based Navigation

3.3.12 Query Mode

Query Mode can be used by the Visually Challenged user to search the website for an input text string. This feature makes the use of Google's "Search within the Site" feature. Code glimpse for the same is shown in the Table 3.9.

```
private void textBox2_KeyDown(object sender, System.Windows.Forms.KeyEventArgs e)
    {
        syn.SpeakAsync((e.KeyData).ToString());
        HtmlDocument doc = webBrowser1.Document;

        if (e.KeyValue == (char)13)
        {
            String srch;
            String str;
            String url = doc.Url.ToString();
            srch = textBox2.Text;
        str = "www.google.com/search?q=" + srch + "&sitesearch=" + url;
            if (!str.StartsWith("http://") &&
            !str.StartsWith("https://"))
            {
                str = "http://" + str;
            }

            webBrowser1.Navigate(str);
            textBox1.Text = str;
        }
    }
```

Table 3.9: Query mode of WACTA

3.3.13 Analytical Mode

This mode speaks out the page statistics of the web page e.g. Title, Headings, Domain, Background color, links, image Alt text etc. This gives the visually challenged user the context of the webpage very quickly. The code snippet for the same is shown in Table 3.10.

37

```
private void buttonInteract_Click(object sender, EventArgs e)
    {
        // Step I:  Speak the Title of the Document
        syn.Speak("Title of this webpage is");
        syn.Speak(webBrowser1.DocumentTitle);
        // Step I:  Speak the Domain of the Document for security purpose
        syn.Speak("Domain of this webpage is");
        syn.Speak(webBrowser1.Document.Domain);
        // Step II: Speak the Background colorof the webpage
        syn.Speak("Background Color of this webpage is set to");
        syn.Speak(webBrowser1.Document.BackColor.ToString());
        // Step III: Speak the <H1> Elements of the webpage
        HtmlElementCollection theElementCollection1;
        theElementCollection1 =
webBrowser1.Document.GetElementsByTagName("H1");
        syn.Speak("These are the Headings of the webpage");
        foreach (HtmlElement curElement in theElementCollection1)
        {

            if (curElement.InnerText != null)
            {
                syn.Speak((curElement.InnerText.ToString()));

            }

        }
        syn.Speak("Number of Links on this web page are");
        syn.Speak(webBrowser1.Document.Links.Count.ToString());

    }
```

Table 3.10: Analytic mode of WACTA

3.3.14 Text Glimpse Mode

This mode is useful for users having low vision due to which they may not read the text on webpage without difficulty. Although, they can view the web page and its various regions but this mode allows user to right click on some point of screen and if there is some text underlying the point, it is spoken out by the narrator. Thus, the user with low vision can get his topic of interest without the need to listen sequentially all the text of the web page. The mode has been implemented on ContextMenuShowing event of HtmlDocument class. The handler makes the use of GetElementFromPoint method of HtmlDocument class. The code snippet is shown in Table 3.11

```
private void Document_ContextMenuShowing(Object sender, HtmlElementEventArgs e)
    {
        if (webBrowser1.Document != null)
        {
            HtmlElement elem =
webBrowser1.Document.GetElementFromPoint(e.ClientMousePosition);
            if (elem != null && elem.InnerText != null)
            {
                syn.Speak(elem.InnerText.ToString());
            }
        }
    }
```

```
webBrowser1.Document.ContextMenuShowing += new
HtmlElementEventHandler(Document_ContextMenuShowing);
```

Table 3.11: Text Glimpse Mode of WACTA

3.3.15 Narrator Voice Management

The WACTA browser makes use of SpeechSynthesizer class to narrate the web page elements in the controlled and desired order. A single instance of this class has been used throughout the System to avoid the multiple voice output streams which may create confusion. Various methods of SpeechSynthesizer class have been used to enable changes in voice characteristics of narrator like volume, rate, pitch, gender etc. These methods have been implemented on the handler of PreviewKeyDown event of WebBrowser Class. The code snippet is shown in Table 3.12.

39

```
void webBrowser1_PreviewKeyDown(object sender, PreviewKeyDownEventArgs e)
    {

        if (e.KeyCode == Keys.Left)
        {
            if (syn != null && syn.Rate > -10)
                syn.Rate--;
        }

        if (e.KeyCode == Keys.Right)
        {
            if (syn != null && syn.Rate < 10)
                syn.Rate++;
        }
        if (e.KeyCode == Keys.Escape)
        {

            syn.SpeakAsyncCancelAll();

        }

        if (e.KeyCode == Keys.ControlKey)
        {

            syn.Pause();

        }

        if (e.KeyCode == Keys.Space)
        {

            syn.Resume();

        }

    }
```

Table 3.12: Narrator Voice Management in WACTA

3.3.16 Speech Feedback for User Inputs

To avoid unreliability and malfunctioning of the system, speech recognition module is not included in this framework. Only keyboard based input with speech feedback to the key presses is the requirement for the Internet surfing by a visually challenged.

40

```
private void textBox1_KeyDown(object sender, System.Windows.Forms.KeyEventArgs e)
    {

        syn.SpeakAsync((e.KeyData).ToString());

    }
```

```
this.textBox1.KeyDown += new
System.Windows.Forms.KeyEventHandler(this.textBox1_KeyDown);
```

Table 3.13: Speech Feedback Management in WACTA

3.3.17 Commands and Key Shortcuts in WACTA

Table 3.14 lists various commands and key shortcuts assigned to the WACTA web browser. Fig. 3.4 shows a snapshot of WACTA web browser.

Fig 3.4: The *WACTA* Browser

Keyboard Command	Usage
Tab	Forward Navigate to the next focusable element on the Web page.
Shift + Tab	Backward Navigate to the previous focusable element on the Web page.
↓ (Down)	Forward Navigate to the next HTML element on the Web page.
↑ (Up)	Backward Navigate to the previous HTML element on the Web page.
→ (Right)	Increment the speaking rate of the narrator voice.
← (Left)	Decrement the speaking rate of the narrator voice.
Control	Pause the speaking of the narrator.
Escape	Cancel all the speaking of the narrator.
Space Bar	Resume the speaking of the narrator.
Alt + L	Go to the Address (Location) Bar of Web browser.
Alt + G	Activate the Glimpse Mode.
Alt+ N	Activate the News style Mode.
Alt + A	Activate the Analysis Mode.
Alt + I	Activate the Interactive Mode.
Alt + Q	Activate the Query within the Website Mode.

Table 3.14: Lists of Keyboard Commands in *WACTA*

3.4 USER EVALUATION OF WACTA

The prototype designed complies with the W3C's User Agent Accessibility Guidelines (UAAG). The prototype is already tested for 25 skilled Visually Challenged users and they have found it user friendly as it fulfills their basic requirements to access the internet effectively for both routine and important tasks. Details of evaluation methodology and its results are discussed in Chapter 7.

3.5 CONCLUSIONS

It can be concluded that WACTA web browser fulfills the basic requirements of Visually Challenged users to access the internet effectively for both routine and important tasks. The design and development of the WACTA web browser is a step forward in the direction of providing an effective yet affordable web accessibility solution for Visually Challenged users.

CHAPTER 4
DIRECT SPEECH-ENABLING THE PUBLIC UTILITY WEBSITES

4.1 INTRODUCTION

Despite many assistive tools available for browsing the web, visually challenged users are not able to perform the tasks using internet that are done by persons without such disability. There are important tasks like getting a berth booked on Railways Reservation Website, deposit tax etc that are complex in nature and have span about multiple web pages. Such task may not be conveniently performed by a visually challenged using assistive technologies like screen readers. Besides, the assistive tools may not be installed on a public terminal. This makes a disadvantage since the web based facility for such public utilities is even more required for visually challenged users than their visually able counterparts. In this context, we have provided a framework SICE (Speech Interface For Client Environment) using which, owners of the public utility websites may directly speech enables their existing websites for more important functionalities at a minimum cost and effort required. The framework makes use of existing technologies like JavaScript and speech API, therefore provides robust and lightweight solution to the accessibility problem. . As a case study, we demonstrate the usefulness of the proposed framework by showing its working on a key functionality of the Indian Railways website.

4.2 SYSTEM DESIGN AND ARCHITECTURE
4.2.1   Design Goals and Decisions

The goal is to design a framework which will facilitate the owner of website to provide a speech interface for the visually disabled. The framework should be based on providing an alternate access system on the fly using one single website so that the overheads involved are minimal. It should be scalable i.e. can be expanded for additional functionalities over time. Accessibility, Usability and Navigability should be enhanced considerably. Access time/ Usage time for a given task should be reduced. Instances of confusion or indecisiveness during navigation should be eliminated completely. The system should be able to run for secure connections or at least in a mix of secure and insecure connection with extra measures of security through providing restricted access to the alternate speech based system.

Local installations should not be required. Thus, user should be able to access and use the website from any public terminal. However, it should seamlessly work with screen reader like JAWS if available, without any conflict. To avoid unreliability during the system use, no speech recognition module is added. Only speech synthesis for the text on the web and voice feedback for keyboard operations is required by a visually disabled to use the web.

4.2.2 The Conceptual Architecture

To provide an alternate interface for visually disabled on websites of public interest with the goals stated previous section, we have designed a framework that makes use of JavaScript and dynamic contents to improve the accessibility and usability through their power of controlling the tasks on the user computer [27]. The framework is inspired by the WebAnyWhere, with two notable differences: First, in the proposed system, the speech based interface shall be provided by the first party i.e. the owner of the website rather than by a third party as is the case with WebAnyWhere. Second, our predefined task based approach enforces strict ordering of elements to be spoken and this ordering is priory known to the server. The framework is based on the "attach on request" concept. Thus, it makes the use of one single site to provide the speech based interface on the fly without affecting its normal course for the users without visual disability.

SpeechEnabler is the core of this framework. It is implemented as a web server plug-in. The SpeechEnabler acts like a macro recorder which records and saves the sequence of page/form elements (hereafter called 'the active nodes') to be visited to perform a given task in the form of executable code on the server. Thus, on the website to be speech enabled for some functionality, the developer has to simply traverse along the page elements in the desired sequence. The SpeechEnabler records the active nodes with their order of traversal in the form of a macro. A key shortcut is designated on the home page of the original site to make a request for accessing the functionality by the visually disabled. On user request through the designated key shortcut for the task, the macro on the server is triggered; it adds the client side JavaScript code on the response page(s) on the fly to build a logical chain among active nodes in the desired sequence along which user can control the traversal to perform the designated task. In addition, it attaches the sever side interface with the speech server to speak out the details of the currently focused form element and voice feedback of keyboard operations. The complete process has been described pictorially in fig. 4.1 and fig. 4.2.

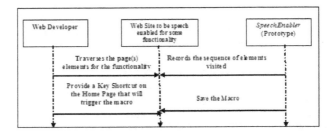

Fig. 4.1: Interactions during the website creation: On an existing website, it requires a little effort to make a functionality speech enabled using *SpeechEnabler.*

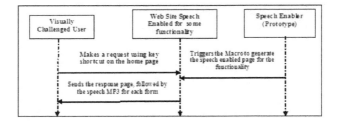

Fig. 4.2: User Initiation: Visually disabled user opts for using the dedicated speech based functionality through a key shortcut request from the home page.

More specifically, on trigger of the macro as a result of user request, the process creates the response page(s) on the fly attaching a unique ID to each relevant element in the order of the traversal in the DOM tree to perform the task. For example, if there are eight active nodes to be traversed in the first page, IDs from 101 to 108 will be assigned to them. Similarly, in the next (second) page, if there are five active nodes to be traversed, IDs from 201 to 205 will be assigned to them and so on. Fixation of IDs to the active nodes in this way ensures the strict ordering of traversal to perform the task and also in pre-fetching the next element to be spoken out. Assignment of IDs also helps in making the focus to an active node which is found to be the source of error during form validation. JavaScript has a remarkable ability of modifying a node in the document structure on the fly.

Interactions of user with the host server and speech server are shown using the conceptual architecture in the fig. 3. Initially, SpeechEnabler contains the application logic (order of traversal among active nodes for the functionality, saved in macro) and speech services (logic to forward the speech request to the speech server) as shown in Fig. 4.3 (a). User request to use the functionality is sent using the designated key shortcut on the homepage. As a result, the relevant macro of the SpeechEnabler is triggered. SpeechEnabler handles the application logic on its own by preparing the response page on the fly and forwards the speech requests to the speech server. This fact is shown in Fig. 4.3(b). Once the page is loaded, command and control is taken by the web browser through the JavaScript code of the page for generating speech output through the speech server for the element in focus. Speech server converts the content of the speech service request forwarded by the browser into the speech MP3 and streams it to the user as part of response. This process is shown in Fig. 4.3(c).

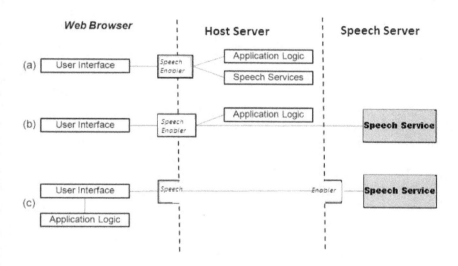

Fig. 4.3: Interactions among User, Host Server and Speech Server during the website usage

In the proposed system, the order of the page/form elements to be focused and spoken is made definite and predefined. The speech server sends the speech mp3 for a form element, currently under focus which is played on the user machine using existing player or plug-in and the user is prompted to enter their details. Meanwhile, speech for the next element in the order is pre-fetched. Focus to the next element in the form is made by the down arrow key press which, at the same time, generates an event on which the pre-fetched speech for the element currently focused is played. Thus, user may control the traversal along the active page elements using up or down arrow keys. On pressing the submit button in a form, if everything is ok, user is taken and focused to the first element of the next related form which is again known priory.

4.3 SPEECH ENABLING PUBLIC UTILITY WEBSITES: CASE STUDY OF INDIAN RAILWAYS WEBSITE

Indian Railways, being fully State controlled, is a major means of local transport in India. At present, Indian Railways provides various services viz. enquiry, online reservation, tour planning & management and hotel booking through its exclusive website, i.e. www.irctc.co.in. Prior to this service being operational, the travelers had to physically visit the reservation centers to avail the reservation and other services. They had to wait in long queues to get the services. Now, as a convenient choice, a user can avail the service promptly, without making any physical movement, through online access to the Indian Railways Website. A large number of persons are taking advantage of this facility every day.

Unfortunately, this facility is not being availed by approximately seven million visually challenged in the country due to lack of any suitable interface available on the website for them. As compared to their sighted counterparts, they are in more need of such a facility that could empower them by eliminating their physical movement for getting the service from a reservation centre. To take care of security related issues at high priority and to prevent various malpractices & abuses made by agents or others, the site owners have imposed various types of restrictions for using the website or its database. This prevents the use of third party approaches like "WebAnyWhere" to access the site.

The website has several noted instances of inaccessibility where a screen reader user may get trapped during a task e.g. Book a Berth. If this task could be done by providing a separate dialogue based system accessible from the homepage of the Indian Railways website, it would be more than worth making effort for providing such an interface.

4.3.1 Navigation related issues

If the Indian Railways website, stated above is observed, it will be revealed that each web page is divided into many frames. To perform a task e.g. Book a Berth may not be a problem to a sighted person as s/he can always locate the link of interest to proceed forward. But, for a visually challenged, using a screen reader, it may take long time to locate the required link as the screen reader will speak out the links in sequential order. Further, structure of website may also create confusion and situation of indecision. Even some frames may be inaccessible to the screen readers. For example, after

47

submitting the train and class details, the Train details and availability appears just above the previous form "List of Trains" which is inaccessible to the screen reader. Thus, the visually challenged user may be unable to click on 'Book' link (Fig. 7).

A visually challenged user may accidently click a link or picture of an advertisement which may take him/ her away from his website of interest.

4.3.2 Identify the Key functionalities of the website

The first task is to identify the key functionalities on the Indian Railways website, which should be made accessible and usable through a speech based interface. The functionalities may be speech enabled in a phased manner: more important first. To begin with, Book a Berth is a heavily used functionality on the site. Thus, it a good start point to make this functionality speech enabled.

4.3.3 Speech enabling the Book a Berth functionality

The task Book a Berth is fairly complex as a user requires visiting at least Nine different web pages including two pages from a third party (i.e., Bank: to make payment). Each page has several links. Thus, after submitting a form on each page, user has to find the next page element of interest on his/her own as the control does not automatically redirect to the next desired page element. To speech enable the task Book a Berth as per our plan, the order of traversal of the active nodes is recorded by the SpeechEnabler in a macro on the host server. User request through the designated key shortcut triggers the relevant macro on the server. On the response page, SpeechEnabler assigns a unique ID to each active node in sequential order and adds the JavaScript code to establish a close chain among these active nodes. On the server side, it attaches the necessary code to interact with speech API. The response page is sent to the user along with the speech mp3 in sequential order of the active nodes.

The working of the speech enabled functionality Book a Berth may be demonstrated using the following scenario. Here, it is assumed that the Visually challenged user makes the use of down arrow keys to focus the next active nodes after filling the value for the current input.

1. Home Page (Fig. 4.4)
   a. Visually Challenged user presses the designated Functionality Key for *Book a Berth*
   b. Control transfers to "Login Form"
   c. System speaks: User Name, Text Box.
   d. User enters his user name, listens his key presses in the text box currently in focus.
   e. System speaks: Password, Text Box.

  f. User enters his Password, listens his key presses in the text box currently in focus.

  g. System speaks: Login, Submit Button.

  h. On user click, Control transfers to linked page at "Plan My Travel" Form.

2. Plan My Travel Page (Fig. 4.5)

  a. System speaks: From, Text Box.

  b. User enters the code for Source Station, listens his key presses in the text box currently in focus.

  c. System speaks: To, Text Box.

  d. User enters the code for Destination Station, listens his key presses in the text box currently in focus.

  e. System speaks: Date, Date Table Object.

  f. System speaks the Headers (Month name) from each table of months,

  g. User clicks the month name in the table header currently in focus.

  h. System speaks each date of the selected Month table sequentially.

  i. User clicks the desired date in the table currently in focus.

  j. System speaks: Ticket Type, Option Button.

  k. System speaks options for Ticket Type, sequentially.

  l. User clicks the desired Ticket Type in the Option Button currently in focus.

  m. System speaks: Quota, Option Button.

  n. System speaks options for Quota, sequentially.

  o. User clicks the desired Quota Type in the Option Button currently in focus.

  p. System speaks: Find Trains, Submit Button.

  q. On user click, Control transfers to linked page at "List of Trains" Page.

3. List of Trains Page (Fig. 4.6)

  a. System speaks: List of Trains, Option Button.

  b. System speaks options for Trains and berth availability.

  c. User clicks the desired Train & Class in the Option Button currently in focus.

  d. On user click, Control transfers to the page having "Train Details".

4. Train Details Page (Fig. 4.7)

  a. System speaks: Availability, Table with Links.

  b. System speaks the table data sequentially for date, availability and Link for "Book."

  c. User clicks the "Book" link on the desired date currently in focus.

  d. Control transfers to the "Passenger Details" page

5. Passenger Details Page (Fig. 4.8)

  a. System speaks: Name, Text Box.

  b. User enters his name, listens his key presses in the text box currently in focus.

  c. System speaks: Age, Text Box.

  d. User enters his Age, listens his key presses in the text box currently in focus.

  e. System speaks: Sex, Option Box.

  f. System speaks the Options

    g. User selects his Sex, currently in focus.

    h. System speaks: Berth Preference, Option Box.

    i. System speaks the Options,

    j. User selects his Berth Preference, currently in focus.

    k. System speaks: Senior Citizen, Checkbox.

    l. User checks if eligible, the checkbox currently in focus.

    m. System speaks: Verification Code, Text Box.

    n. System speaks the code.

    o. User enters each character of the code in the text box currently in focus after listening it.

    p. System speaks: Go, Submit Button.

    q. On user click, Control transfers to linked page at "Ticket Details" Page.

6. Ticket Details Page (Fig. 4.9)

    a. System speaks the details of the ticket.

    b. System Speaks: Make Payment, Submit Button.

    c. On user click, Control transfers to the "Make Payment" Page

7. Make Payment Page (Fig. 4.10)

    a. System speaks: Types for Payments, Option Button.

    b. System speaks each available payment type

    c. User clicks the preferred type currently under the focus.

    d. System speaks: Options available, Radio Button.

    e. System speaks the available options for the type of payment selected by the user.

    f. User selects the preferred option under focus. Control transfers to the bank page for payment.

Fig. 4.4: Home Page of www.irctc.co.in

Fig. 4.5: Plan my Travel Page of www.irctc.co.in

Fig. 4.6: List of Trains Page of www.irctc.co.in

Fig. 4.7: Berth Availability Page of www.irctc.co.in

Fig. 4.8: Passenger Details Page of www.irctc.co.in

Fig. 4.9: Ticket Details Page of www.irctc.co.in

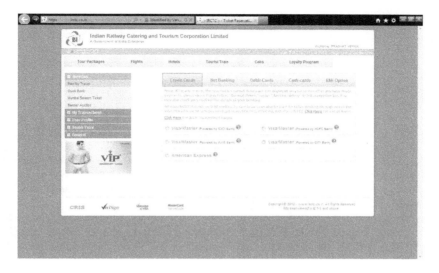

Fig. 4.10: Make Payment Page of www.irctc.co.in

4.4 SYSTEM ASSESSMENT

4.4.1 Results and Discussion

In this chapter, we have outlined an alternative approach for addressing the issue related to usability of the websites of public interest. There are instances of important tasks like the one described by us as a case study, which are difficult to be performed by visually disabled using any of the existing web surfing tools. The proposed framework will provide workable and robust solutions to such complex tasks. Thus, a visually disabled user can perform the task on any available public terminal conveniently. The framework may pose certain challenges as well. For example, on secure websites it may require to restrict the alternative access to the target group by the means of special login IDs or digital signatures.

So far, researchers have been emphasizing on finding the generic solutions to the accessibility issues. Expectations from the web content providers have been limited to providing accessible contents that could be usable with screen readers. Screen Readers most often fail to perform the task due to its own limitations. Traditionally, an industry criterion for making investment on a project has been determined by the number of use cases offered by the aimed product. Thus, working at such a micro level may not gain due importance. Our work is primarily addressed to the responsible owners of the big websites meant for public usage that are accessed heavily. A little effort on their part could help the visually disabled to a great extent. Thus, owners of the websites of public interest should come forward to add provisions for dedicated speech based interfaces for visually disabled.

4.4.2 Conclusions

In this chapter, we highlighted the need and importance of making the websites of public interest speech enabled for offering their important services to the visually disabled and presented a framework for this purpose. These services may be accessed by the visually disabled on any public terminal without having the need for any local installation. The approach is based on providing an alternate access system on the fly from one single site. The framework makes use of existing technologies like JavaScript, available speech APIs etc. Therefore, it provides a lightweight and robust solution to the accessibility problem. A future enhancement in the framework may be suggested where all the page elements except for the active nodes are 'locked' thus allowing the visually disabled only to traverse along the active nodes in a definitive order.

All websites are not accessed equally on the Web. Therefore, it seems important that the websites which account for heavy traffic are made better accessible [28]. Public utility websites should feel a greater sense of responsibility in providing feasible, error free and workable functionality from the point of view of a visually disabled rather than leaving them to struggle with their screen readers. Usability, in its best form, at least for the most important functionalities, must be incorporated by the owners of these websites at the time of design itself. Other functionalities may be added up on the need basis in an incremental way.

It is hoped that the goal of achieving the benefits of internet to all including visually disabled as desired by its original propagators can be achieved to some extent by providing the speech based dedicated functionalities on important websites of public interest.

CHAPTER 5
VOICE-XML /VOIP BASED CLIENT INTERFACE
FOR INTERACTIVE BROWSING

5.1 INTRODUCTION

The Web has become an important medium for delivering information, and more and more people rely on it for work and entertainment. For example, users like to check e-mails, read news, watch videos, listen to music, ticket reservation and do shopping on the Web. An important domain for voice based web applications is to support the blind or people with other disabilities. Voice based interfaces can empower visually challenged people in many ways e.g. seeking information of their interest or making transactions through web. Unfortunately, real scenario is still not satisfactory altogether. Vast power and resources of web are still not usable for this underprivileged group. Many of the tools available do not cater even the basic need of the target group. The reason is lack of control over content access.

VoiceXML has emerged as standard for developing IVRS based telephony applications. It provides the requisite robustness and control over dialogue based delivery over telephone line. Here, we present a framework based on VoiceXML specifications for developing web based interactive voice applications. Communications are made using VOIP; therefore, user does not have the dependency on telephony interface as required by existing VoiceXML specifications. Besides, it is able to handle the complex and voluminous information of web.

5.2 SPEECH-BASED INTERACTIVE SYSTEMS

This section describes the major interactive speech interface frameworks currently available.

5.2.1 VoiceXML

HTML has roots in publishing. VoiceXML has a programming language background. It has the impression of a programming language: control constructs, variables, event handlers, nested scooping, and so on. At the beginning, VoiceXML was designed to be a programming language easy to learn, lightweight and interpreted for developing VUIs. VoiceXML renders content as speech and interacts with the user using speech recognition and speech synthesis technologies. The way of Voice XML structures for interaction with user is dialogs. A dialog consists of a sequence of prompts spoken by the computer and responses spoken by a person. Responses are given by the person by voice command or key using a keypad. In contrast with GUI windows which are multitasked and two dimensional, VUI Dialogs are sequential and linear by nature. Architecturally, VoiceXML interfaces are event-driven interfaces like GUIs. In a dialog, the computer speaks a prompt and then waits for the user to respond to it. The computer waits until a speech recognition event occurs. A speech recognition event is initiated by the speech recognition engine, which continuously analyzes the user's speech and attempts to match it to expected responses in the dialog. There are a lot of possible speech recognition events, including "recognized responses." "got a responses but didn't recognize it", "no response" and so on. Unlike GUIs and WUIs, where the events that drive the interface are low-level, non-equivocal incidences (button pressed, mouse clicked, and so on), events in VoiceXML interfaces are the result of complex, computation-intensive, possible processing with errors.

5.2.2   GUIs, WUIs, VUIs

GUI, WUI and VUI represent the major markup language-based browsing interfaces to the internet. GUI is the most fully developed of the three is exemplified by products such as Netscape Communicator and Microsoft Internet Explorer. WUI, the most next developed interfaces, is implemented by "micro browsers" embedded in wireless phones and personal digital assistants (PDAs). VUIs (Voice User Interfaces) are just beginning to appear as browsing interfaces to the internet, and they are driven by the standardization of VoiceXML 1.0. The markup languages for these three types of interfaces are all based on XML. XML is a Markup Meta Language derived from SGML. XML simplifies some of the complex and little-used features of SGML, but it still provides a flexible and extensible base for defining specialized markup languages.

5.2.3   W3C recommended Speech Interface Framework

- **VoiceXML 2.0** is designed for creating audio dialogs that feature synthesized speech, digitized audio, recognition of spoken and DTMF key input, recording of spoken input, telephony, and mixed initiative conversations [29]. Its major goal is to bring the advantages of Web-based development and content delivery to interactive voice response applications.
- **VoiceXML 2.1** specifies a set of features commonly implemented by Voice Extensible Markup Language platforms, with a small set of widely implemented additional features like Referencing Scripts Dynamically, Using <mark> to Detect Barge-in During Prompt Playback, Using <data> to Fetch XML Without Requiring a Dialog Transition, <data> Fetching Properties, Using <foreach> to Concatenate Prompts and Loop through Executable Content etc [30].
- **Voice Browser Call Control (CCXML)** is designed to provide telephony call control support for dialog systems, such as VoiceXML [35]. While CCXML can be used with any dialog systems capable of handling media, CCXML has been designed to complement and integrate with a VoiceXML interpreter.

- **State Chart XML (SCXML)** provides a generic state-machine based execution environment based on CCXML and Harel State Tables. .
- **Speech Recognition Grammar Specification (SRGS) 1.0** [38], This document defines syntax for representing grammars for use in speech recognition so that developers can specify the words and patterns of words to be listened for by a speech recognizer. The syntax of the grammar format is presented in two forms, an Augmented BNF Form and an XML Form. The specification makes the two representations mappable to allow automatic transformations between the two forms.
- **Semantic Interpretation (SISR) 1.0,** Semantic Interpretation for Speech Recognition offers semantic interpretation tags that can be added to speech recognition grammars to compute information to return to an application on the basis of rules and tokens that were matched by the speech recognizer [32].
- **Speech Synthesis Markup Language (SSML) 1.0 and 1.1,** The Speech Synthesis Markup Language Specification is one of the standards and is designed to provide a rich, XML-based markup language for assisting the generation of synthetic speech in Web and other applications [30]. The essential role of the markup language is to provide authors of synthesizable content a standard way to control aspects of speech such as pronunciation, volume, pitch, rate, etc. across different synthesis-capable platforms.
- **Pronunciation Lexicon Specification (PLS) 1.0** provides the syntax for specifying pronunciation lexicons to be used by Speech Recognition and Speech Synthesis.

5.2.4 Other Framework for speech Interface

- **SUIML (Speech User Interface Markup Language),** is eXtended Markup Language XML) application [31] that specifies conversations between man and machine [32]. A SUIML document describes a set of objects that represent almost all the information needed in a conversation except for grammars.
- **VoiceBuilder** [35], is framework for building speech applications with no programming effort, based on a markup language and an algorithm using code templates. It was able to generate fully functional speech applications using both system initiative and mixed initiative dialogue strategies. It is a type of Interactive Development Environment(IDE)
- **Web Access by Voice (WAV)** [36], is the integration of many different technologies such as automatic speech recognition, scripts for web navigation, text to speech conversion, with a novel way of extracting information from web via voice in a programmatic manner. This is a utility which provides voice interface on Operating Systems.
- **CoScripter**[37], is a programming by demonstration solution, which helps the blind user perform a pre-define internet task more efficiently. Overall, it is a task oriented voice interface.

- **Spoken Dialogue System (SDS)** [38], is designed for providing automatic dialogue-based voice services accessible through telephone like VoiceXML effectively. It works same as VoiceXML.
- **SpeechPa** [39], is an intelligent speech interface for PA (Personal Assistant) in research and development projects.
- **WebAnima** [40], is a web-based embodied conversational assistant agent which provides conversational interface and ontologies that support semantic interpretation.
- **GeoVAQA** [41], is a restricted Domain Spoken Question Answering system in the scope of the Spanish geography. The system consists of a web based application that allows speech recognition based on HMM model and sends back a concise textual answer.
- **A Voice-Activated Web-based Mandarin Chinese Spoken Document Retrieval System** [42], is an integrated technology for both spoken document retrieval and voice-activated WWW browser with a specific type of speech recognition technique specially design for Chinese language.
- **Florence** [43], a dialogue manager with a more general approach that uses an extensible and flexible framework to combine interchangeable and interoperable dialogue strategies as appropriate to the task. Florence's declarative XML-based language facilitates the development of natural language applications and allows the dialogue author to encapsulate and reuse different algorithms between applications.

Overall, it is clear from the above list that a slew of different XML instances are currently being developed with the goal of making the Web voice-enabled. The attention seems to be centered on developing a language in which the website developer or Voice-Web service provider can specify how the user can access Web content. In other words, it is up to the developer to create an XML specification of the speech-based interaction that a user can have with the server. VoiceXML is emerging as the standard and essentially subsumes SpeechML in functionality. VoiceXML provides the programmer with the ability to specify an XML document that defines the types of commands a voice-enabled system can receive and the text that a voice-enabled system can synthesize. Similar to the Java Speech Markup Language, it allows the XML programmer to specify the attributes used to render a given excerpt of text. This may include information about parameters such as rate and volume. Beyond that, VoiceXML, VoXML, and TalkML provide the infrastructure to define dialogues between the user and the system.

5.3 DESIGN OF SICE FRAMEWORK

This section describes the major design decisions and design structure of SICE framework.

5.3.1   Enhanced Functionality

The W3C speech interface framework incorporates Voice eXtensible Markup Language (VoiceXML or VXML), speech synthesis markup language (SSML), Speech Recognition Grammar Specification (SRGS), voice browser Call Control XML (CCXML) and Semantic Interpretation for Speech Recognition (SISR). VoiceXML controls how applications interact with a user through interactive voice response over telephone lines; the SRGS offers support for speech recognition; the CCXML provides telephony call control support and other dialog systems, while the SISR defines how speech grammars bind to application semantics [44]. These are able to handle small information via telephone but when the amount of information is in huge quantity and bears complex structure, telephony voice user interface becomes a frustrating tool for user. Being an enhancement over VoiceXML, SICE Framework may be used to design and develop both telephony-based as well as web-based speech interfaces.

5.3.2   Platform and Language

Microsoft Windows 7 has been the chosen operating system for this due to its popularity and wide acceptance. Further, due to flexibility provided by it in the development of applications, .Net platform with C# language has been used for development of prototype SICE Framework. Microsoft Language Interface provides better interface in term of functionality and processing power.

5.3.3   System Architecture

The detailed schematic diagram and Structure of framework is shown in fig 5.1 and fig 5.2 respectively. Emphasis is given on better Human-Computer Interaction (HCI) and ease of use through controlled output so that user feels a pleasant experience even during handling interactions of complex nature. The aim is also centered on saving time and efforts in getting information of interest.

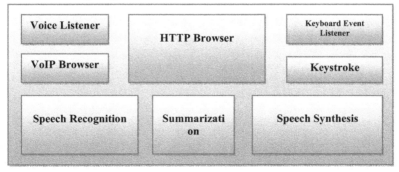

Fig 5.1: Schematic Diagram

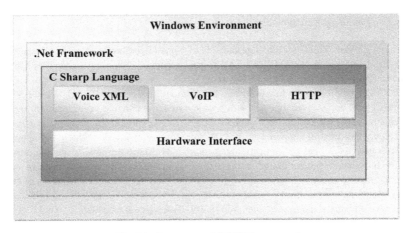

Fig 5.2: Structure of SICE Framework

In the following subsections, we describe the main components of SICE with their role and responsibilities in details.

5.3.3.1   HTTP Event Handler

HTTP handles the response made from the request in the form of voice that passes through VoIP Interface and the response in the form of request webpage. It follows the following algorithm after taking request from user over Voice:

[Assume "|"= OR and URL=Uniform Resource Locator; Request send through VoIP]
[HTTP Event Handler]
Start
Request Page= absoluteURL | abs_path (getting from Speech to Text Conversion on speech server)
Response   = Status-Line;
(General-Header;| Response-Header;| Entity-Header);
                              CRLF [Entity-Body];
Interpret the Response and check validity of page
If (Page is Valid)
Display the content in the form of HTML on browser.
Else
Shown Message "Some Error on requested webpage"
End
[Response Buffer=NULL]

5.3.3.2   VoIP Event Handler

This module provides two way communications over the internet in a way similar to telephone talk. SICE Framework makes the use of VoIP to take the voice from client side to server side in order to perform processing and returns the response from Speech Synthesizer to HTTP Handler.

5.3.3.3   Keystroke Handler

Keystroke is the event occurred when a key is presses on keyboard or similar device. The Key stroke handler module generates and processes the request to server similar to VoIP handler when a keystroke occurs.

5.3.3.4   Speech Recognizer

The speech recognizer resides on server side and always remains in listening mode. However, it is triggered to recognition mode only when a specified word with fixed threshold frequency is occurred. The speech recognition process follows five steps [30]

a. Audio input: The human voice is transmitted through a microphone connected to a PC with help of standard sound card. The recommended microphone must have the noise cancellation feature so that the actual voice with minimum background noise is received by the speech server.

b. Acoustic processor: The acoustic processor filters out background noise again and converts the captured audio into a series of phonemes.

c. Word matching: The System attempts to match the sounds to the most-likely words in two ways. First, it uses acoustical analysis to build a list of possible matches that contain similar sounds. Then, it uses language modeling (the likelihood that a given word appears between those coming before and after it) to narrow the list to the best candidates. In addition, the word-matching process draws on the user-defined domain (the set of vocabularies, pronunciations, and word-usage models, as well as a model of the user's speech and words). The user can extend the domain by adding new words and can create multiple domains for different applications. Finally, continuous-speech SR examines contextual information to predict what words should come next in the current phrase. This also helps the system to distinguish among homonyms.

d. Decoder: The decoder selects the most-likely word based on the rankings assigned during word matching and assembles the word along with those selected earlier into the most-likely sentence combination.

e. Text output: This module sends the text transcription directly into a separate word processing program which prepares it for the next phase.

5.3.3.5   *Speech Synthesizer*

This part of SICE Framework resides on server side providing output (response) over client side in speech form. It works with natural voice especially in Indian context.

5.3.3.6   *Content Summarizer*

This component provides the control over the output text content based on the summarized text and keywords extracted from the document using an algorithm based on term co-occurrence. The algorithm is mentioned below and process shown in fig 5.3.

Generate the terms set by removing the meaningless words like articles, preposition etc.
Calculate the frequency of each term or word and select the first n words.
Maximum(n)<=Total no of different words calculated in current document
Calculate set of co-occurred word.
Generate a Logical graph G = (V,E), where V=first n words and E=set of co-occurred words.
Create cluster based on frequency ranking or in equal size
Extract subject term using, Subject Term = $\sum_{w,w' \in E(G')} C(w, w')$

Where C(w,w') = R(w|w') /2 + R(w'|w) /2
And R(w|w') =f(w,w') / f(w'') ,where f(w,w') is the number of co-occurrences of terms, and f(w') is number of occurrences of w'.
Generate the summarized text based on term co-occurrence graph.
Convert text in VoiceXML format by inserting <tag></tag> for a paragraph if occurred

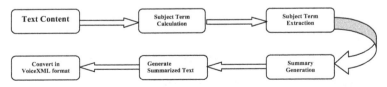

Fig 5.3: Summarization Algorithm Process

5.3.3.7   *Interface*

It integrates the Hardware components i.e. Keyboard, Microphone and Speaker with the SICE Browser so that user can listen and browser can recognize speech and process it by sending request via SICE Browser.

5.3.3.8   *Encrypter-Decrypter*

This component is an added security feature in SICE Framework, which provide secure way of transaction/Voice over HTTP and VoIP either in the way of Voice or Text or Keystroke.

5.4   SPEECH BASED WEB APPLICATIONS DEVELOPMENT USING SICE FRAMEWORK

SICE Framework is good at developing speech based web applications that provide specific functionality to target group e.g. visually challenged. Making query for seat availability/PNR status or exam result may be few such examples. Important is to identify and incorporate those functionalities of the website which would help the target group in substantial way. The working of an application built using SICE framework is demonstrated in the following subsection.

5.4.1   As a Result Checker

When user says "University Result" (keyword already stored for the URL of this page) in front of SICE Browser, this request is recognized by the Speech Server via VoIP.

As the keyword "University Result" is recognized by server, an event is generated which makes request to actual server of HBTI Website to fetch the required webpage and converts it into VoiceXML format for further processing. The requested page is sent to the user in HTML format also.

In the response user speaks the digit of their roll number as "one, two, three, four, five, six, seven, eight, nine, ten". These digits are recognizing on server that provides input to requested page "University Result".

When all required input is provided then SICE server sends request for the relevant page to University server for result and the result page, after converted into VoiceXML, is sent to the user along with the HTML file. Thus, it starts speaking out the result in a predefined format e.g. "You have obtained 65 marks out of 100 in Data Structures". Figure 5.4 - 5.7 illustrate the process.

Fig 5.4: Requested Page

```
1
2   <html>
3   <head>
4   <title>:: HBTI, KANPUR ::</title>
5   <style>
6   a:link{COLOR: #666666; TEXT-DECORATION: none}
7   a:visited{COLOR: #666666; TEXT-DECORATION: none}
8   a:active{COLOR: #666666; TEXT-DECORATION: none}
9   a:hover{COLOR: #666666; TEXT-DECORATION: underline}
10  .s1{font-family: 'Courier New'; font-size:12px}
11  </style>
12  </head>
13  <body topmargin="0" leftmargin="0" style="font family: Verdana; font size:
    8pt; background-image: url('watermark.jpg'); background-repeat: no-repeat;
    background-attachment: fixed; background-position: center">
14  <table align='center' border='0' cellpadding='0' cellspacing='0'
    style='border-collapse: collapse' width='780' height=100%>
15  <tr><td height=96% align=center><BR><BR>
16  <B><u>HBTI Results Odd Semester 2010-11</u></B><BR><BR><table border="1"
    cellpadding="0" cellspacing="0" width="50%" style="border-collapse:
    collapse; font-size: 11px"><FORM METHOD="get" name="f1"><tr><td> Roll
    No. : </td><td><input type="text" name="rollno" maxlength="12" size="20"
    style="font-size: 10px"></td><td><input type="button"
    onClick="document.f1.submit()" size="20" value="Submit" style="font-size:
    10px"></td></tr></FORM></table>
```

Fig 5.5: Source Code for Requested Page

65

```vxml
<vxml version="2.1">
  <form id="MainMenu">
    <field name="RollNumber">
      Please say your roll number.
      <!-- grammar -->
      <grammar type="text/gsl">
        <![CDATA[
          ;Match one of the enclosed digits
          {
            one two three four five six seven eight nine zero
          }
        ]]>
      </grammar>

      <!-- when user was silent, restart the field -->
      <noinput>
        I did not hear anything.  Please try again.
        <reprompt/>
      </noinput>
      <!-- The user said something that was not defined in our grammar -->
      <nomatch>
        I did not recognize that character.  Please try again.
        <reprompt/>
      </nomatch>
    </field>
    <filled namelist="RollNumber">
      <if cond="RollNumber == 'one'">
        <prompt>one entered.</prompt>
      ....................................
      <elseif cond="RollNumber == 'zero'"/>
        <prompt>zero entered.</prompt>
      <else/>
        <prompt>
          A match has occurred, but no specific if statement
          was written for it.
```

Fig 5.6: VoiceXML File of Requested Page

HBTI Results Odd Semester 2010-11

Name:	SHIVAM GUPTA
Father's Name:	SHAILENDRA KUMAR GUPTA
Roll No:	0704586017
Semester :	SEMESTER - 7
Course/Branch:	B. Tech. Leather Technology
Institute Name	Harcourt Butler Technological Institute,Kanpur

MARKS DETAIL

Subject Name	Max. Marks			Marks Obtained		
	Examination	Sessional	Total	Examination	Sessional	Total
Instrumentation and Process Control [TCH706]	100	50	150	30	18	48*
Chemical Reaction Engineering [TCH707]	100	50	150	10	20	30*
Processing of Leather I [TLT701]	100	50	150	73	37	110
Tannery Effluent Treatment [TLT702]	100	50	150	79	40	119
Enterpreneurship Development Programme [ELE-OP]	100	50	150	62	36	98
Leather Processing Lab II [TLT751]	60	40	100	52	30	82
Project (Team Work) [TLT752]	0	50	50	-	38	38
Industrial Training [TLT753]	0	50	50	-	39	39
General Proficiency [GP701]		50	50		44	44

CARRY OVER PAPER	TCH706,TCH707,
RESULTS	CP(2)
TOTAL MARKS	608

1) Although utmost care has been exercised in preparation of marks yet if at any stage any error is detected based on facts; these marks will be treated as null and void and fresh factual marks would be given.
2) If it is detected at any stage that a student appeared in the examination in violation of admission /examination rules/norms, the statement of marks given herein will be treated as null and void.

Fig 5.7: Final Page after providing the required input

66

5.5 CONCLUSIONS

The SICE framework presented in this chapter can be used for design and development of speech based web supporting applications. Advantages are manifold: It provides flexibility like IVRS without requiring telephony. Complex web data can be conveniently handled using customized two way dialogue based access system in a controlled way. The framework is more effective in developing speech based web access systems for dedicated functionalities rather than developing generalized speech interfaces. Website providers themselves can use the framework to provide speech based access to the visually challenged selectively for more important functionalities/ portions. The enhanced functionalities shall be a great contribution to the society in general and to the visually challenged in particular.

CHAPTER 6
PERFORMANCE EVALUATION OF INTERNET
ASSISTIVE TOOLS

At present, no formal framework is available to evaluate the performance of assistive tools that are used by blind users to use internet. In this chapter, we present a hierarchical model for quantitative evaluation of assistive tools for blinds. Identifying various performance attributes and Design metrics, we establish relationship among these to obtain the overall performance Index of the assistive tools.

6.1 DEFINING THE FRAMEWORK

Methodology used in the development of model proposed here is inspired by hierarchical model for assessment of quality of object oriented design based software [45]. A general schematic for the performance evaluation of an assistive tool has been shown in the Fig. 6.1. Attributes in higher order of hierarchy affect the overall performance however; it may be difficult to measure them. Thus, we have to move down in hierarchy to get lower order attributes which can be measured through a well defined set of metrics.

6.1.1 Identification of Performance Attributes

Based on the data available from the literature, attributes like HCI Index, User Satisfaction Index, User Frustration Index, Quality of Life Index, Simplification Index and Tool Effectiveness Index were taken as the set of Performance attributes in the model. These attributes affect the overall browsing experience thus are major performance indicators. Table 6.1 summarizes the Performance Attributes with their roles in performance of assistive tool.

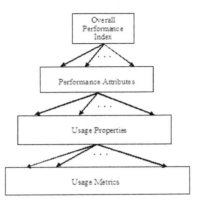

Fig. 6.1: Schematic Hierarchical Structure

Sr. No.	Performance Attribute	Performance Attribute Definition
1	HCI Index	A measure of the extent to which the user interaction with computer is enhanced in comparison to the ground level. It allows the user to comfortably use the assistive tool. It reflects user's control over use of computer.
2	User Satisfaction Index	Reflects the enhancement in user satisfaction level due to the use of the assistive tool in compare to the ground level. It is evident from user applaud for the tool.
3	User Frustration Index	Reflects the reduction in the instances of user's frustration[46] while using the assistive tool in comparison to the ground level.
4	Quality of Life Index	Reflects the gains occurred in the life of blind user and improvement in the ability of a blind in terms of performing tasks independently.
5	Simplification Index	Reflects the extent to which page structure and contents are simplified by the tool.
6	Tool Effectiveness Index	Refers to the assistive tool's ability to achieve the desired functionality and behavior.

Table 6.1: Performance Attribute Definitions

6.1.2   Identification of Usage Properties

A Usage attribute represents an aspect that may affect the performance of assistive tool. We have identified eight Usage Properties that affect the performance attribute in some way or other. The definition of these properties is given in Table 6.2.

Sr. No.	Usage Property	Usage Property Definition
1	Accessibility	Indicates the reduction in no. of unreachable elements in webpage by the use of assistive tool as compare to that in the ground value.
2	Usability	Indicates reduction in difficulty in the use of website. It is denoted by the increase in no of tasks performed from the ground case.
3	Navigability	Indicates the capability to navigate around intra/ inter page links efficiently to access/ use its features.
4	Element Processing Time	Indicates the reduction in average time spent on processing the page elements (nodes) to perform a task using form filling.
5	No. of Probes	Indicates the reduction in average no. of probes [47] required by a blind user after using the assistive tool as compare to the ground case.
6	Page Layout Understandability	Indicates the enhancement in blind user's ability to understand the page layout simplified by assistive tool as compare to the ground case.
7	Page Context Understandability	Indicates the enhancement in blind user's ability to make an overview of the page context [50] as compare to the ground case.
8	Rich Internet Applications (RIA) Understandability	Indicates the enhancement in blind user's ability to understand the RIA content as compare to the ground case [49].

Table 6.2: Usage Property Definitions

6.1.3 Identification of Usage Metrics

Each of the Usage property described in Table 6.3 corresponds to a metric value that is obtained by applying the assistive tool on test case WebPages. The complete suite of Usage Metrics for the proposed model is described in table 6.4.

Sr. No.	Name of the Metric	Metrics Description
1	Accessibility Metric	No. of page elements that can be accessed using keyboard only.
2	Usability Metric	No. of tasks that can be performed on a web page.
3	Navigability Metric	Average no of navigations (Performances) required to access an element on a web page.
4	Time to Process Nodes Metric	Average time spent on an element during form fill to perform a task.
5	probes Metric	Number of probes required on a web page.
6	Structural Assessment Metric	Time required for assessing the layout of a webpage.
7	Context Assessment Metric	Time required for assessing an context/ overview of a webpage.
8	Rich Content Metrics	Number of rich content elements that can be accessed on a web page.

Table 6.3: Usage Metrics Descriptions

6.1.4 Ground Case Values of Usage Metrics

Ground case values of Usage Metrics are obtained when a blind user uses a plain Text To Speech (TTS) to surf the webpage using link navigation through Tab key presses only.

Each of the Usage Property is calculated from the Usage Metric using the following relation:

$$UP = \frac{|\,(UM)_{AT} - (UM)_{GROUND}\,|}{UM}$$

Where UP is the Usage Property, $(UM)_{AT}$ is the Usage Metric value for blind user using assistive tool. $(UM)_{GROUND}$ is the Usage Metric value for blind user in ground case. UM is the corresponding Usage Metric value for sighted user.

6.1.5 Mapping Usage Properties to Performance Attributes

Each Performance Attributes is determined by some of the usage Properties. The Table 6.4 shows the influence of each of the Usage Property on the Performance attributes. An up arrow symbol (↑) indicates that the Usage Metric has positive influence on the Performance Attribute and the down arrow symbol (↓) indicates that the Usage Metric has negative influence on the Performance Attribute.

6.1.6 Formulation for Performance Attributes

For preparation of formulation for Performance Attributes in terms of the Usage Properties, the relative significance of Usage Properties that influence a Performance Attribute has to be weighted proportionally so that the computed values of all Performance Attributes have the same range. A range of 0 to +1 or −1 is selected for the computed values of the Performance Attributes.

Because actual metric values of different ranges are combined in the computation of the Performance Attribute indices, the metric values have to be also normalized. These normalized values of the Usage Metrics are to be then used for computation of the Performance attribute values as per the formulation shown in table

6.1.7 Formulation for Overall Performance Measure of Assistive Tool

Formulation of the overall performance Index of the assistive tool in terms of the Performance attribute values will be based on the relative influence of these attributes on the overall performance of the Assistive Tool. This influence can be determined by aggregating the opinion taken from some specified number of experts. The equation for calculating Overall Performance Index from the Performance attribute values is given in table 6.6. Factor values of C1 to C6 are chosen such that their sum is 1. The values can be set by expert opinion only after considering all the factors discussed previously in section II subsections B, C and D.

	HCI Index	User Satisfaction Index	User Frustration Index	Quality of Life Index	Simplification Index	Tool Effectiveness Index
Accessibility		↑	↓	↑		↑
Usability		↑	↓	↑		↑
Navigability	↑	↑	↓	↑		
Element Processing Time	↓		↑			↓
No. of Probes	↓		↑			↓
Page Layout Understandability	↑	↑			↑	↑
Page Context Understandability		↑	↓	↑	↑	
Rich Content Metrics		↑		↑		↑

Table 6.4: Mapping of Usage Properties to Performance Attributes

Performance Attribute	Formulation for Index Computation
HCI Index	0.75* Navigability +0.75*Page Layout Understandability - 0.25*Element Processing Time-0.25* Number of Probes
User Satisfaction Index	0.10* Accessibility+ 0.20* Usability +0.10* Navigability +0.20*Page Layout Understandability +0.20* Rich Content Metrics +0.20* Page Content Understandability
User Frustration Index	-0.5 * Accessibility- 0.5 * Usability -0.5 * Navigability + 0.5*Element Processing Time-0.5 * Page Content Understandability+0.5* Number of Probes
Quality of Life Index	0.20* Accessibility+ 0.20* Usability + 0.20* Navigability + 0.20* Page Content Understandability+0.20* Rich Content Metrics
Simplification Index	0.5*Page Layout Understandability + 0.5 * Page Content Understandability
Tool Effectiveness Index	0.5* Accessibility+ 0.5* Usability +0.5*Page Layout Understandability +0.5* Rich Content Metrics-0.5* Number of Probes - 0.5*Element Processing Time

Table 6.5: Formulation for the Performance Attributes

Overall Performance Index = C1* HCI Index + C2 *   User Satisfaction Index + C3 * User Frustration Index + C4 * Quality of Life Index + C5 * Simplification Index + C6 * Tool Effectiveness Index

Table 6.6: Equation for Overall Performance Measure

6.1.8   Using the Framework in Performance Evaluation

To use the framework for performance evaluation of assistive tools, following are the desirables:

1. Automated tools to assess the webpage metrics,

2. Benchmark Test cases chosen from each category of webpage defined earlier in section II subsection B. ,
3. A predefined no. of sighted and blind users to run test cases.
4. A predefined no. of experts to Design and run test cases.

It is worth mention that rich work is available related to the accessibility and usability testing of websites [47, 50]. In most cases, the work can be extended for the evaluation of assistive tools.

6.2 CONCLUSIONS

In this chapter, we have tried to formulate a hierarchical framework to evaluate the performance of assistive tools for blind users through carefully chosen performance attributes and indicators. The task was difficult due to lack of related previous work. Although the framework may further require being refined and fine-tuned, it may be the basis for the selection of an assistive tool for blinds. Specifically, our contributions in this regard include:

1. Identification of a ground case that is taken as reference benchmark to evaluate the assistive tools for blinds,
2. Defining the Performance Attributes for assistive tools.
3. Defining Usage properties for assistive tools,
4. Defining the Usage Metrics that are affected by an assistive tool,
5. Establishing relationships between Usage Properties and Performance Attributes thereby getting the overall performance index for the assistive tool for blinds.

It has been common practice to identify a web assistive tool by its distinctive feature or approach e.g. context driven, semantic driven, Annotation based etc. Whatever approach, methodology or strategy used therein, their objective is single: empowering the blind users for what their counterpart sighted users enjoy naturally in day-to-day life. Thus, it is legitimate to formulate the performance evaluation criteria for assistive tools despite several hindrances like diversity in architecture and methodologies, approaches, testability due to lack of well defined benchmark test cases etc. It is expected that these and other issues shall be taken up with priority by the concerned researchers, interest groups and formal bodies in near future.

CHAPTER 7
RESULTS AND DISCUSSION

7.1 INTRODUCTION

An Enhanced Web Browser WACTA has been designed and developed as a part of this research work for visually challenged users, with improved HCI features. The prototype designed complies with the W3C's User Agent Accessibility Guidelines (UAAG). Following are the distinct features of the WACTA web browser:

a. Completely developed using .NET managed code only. Thus, reliability and security are enhanced through automatic garbage collection, automatic bound check etc.
b. Works for both secure and insecure websites,
c. Works for both direct and proxy server based connections
d. Compatible with Windows 7 operating system.
e. Various available browsing modes ensure informed search to quickly locate the required information.
f. Specialized speech enabled browser having range of functionalities which can be easily extended or enhanced.
g. Provision of Mouse based accessibility for Partially visually challenged users

7.2 EVALUATION METHODOLOGY

A group of 25 visually challenged users was selected for this study. The selected users were trained students of age group 20-35 performing their vocational training and were already using JAWS screen reader. The target group was assigned well defined web related task for various usage categories as given in Table 7.1.

S. No.	Usage Category	Defined Task	Website
1.	Reading News etc.	Navigating Times of India News Web Site	www.Indiatimes.com
2.	Link Navigation	Navigating a website of user's choice	----------
3.	Keyword Search	Search for Ghazals of Jagjit Singh	Google (Google.com)
4.	Making Queries	Query for PNR status of a booked Ticket.	Indian Railways (indianrail.gov.in)
5.	Form Filling	Create a Mail account	Yahoo Mail (mail.yahoo.com)
6.	Mailing	To send a mail to friend	Yahoo Mail (mail.yahoo.com)
7.	Making Transaction	To Book a Berth	Irctc.co.in (Indian Railways)
8.	Social Networking	To read and send posts	Facebook.com Blogspot.com

Table 7.1: Test cases to evaluate the WACTA Webbrowser

7.3 EVALUATION RESULTS

Even though the set of users chosen for evaluation of WACTA is a small, the study produced some distinct observations. Results of this evaluation are summarized in Table 7.2 Following observations can be made from the analysis of this evaluation:

1. Most users (about 95%) were able to perform simple tasks like general web site surfing, reading newspapers, topic search etc.
2. A fair number of users (about 65%) were able to perform simple queries like PNR enquiry and finding road route and simple form filling of single page e.g. creating a mail account.
3. An average number of users (about 50%) were able to perform mailing (sending e-mail to a friend).

4. Only few advance users (About 10%) could perform complex task like Transaction for Booking a Berth. The Social Sites like Facebook were not fully usable due to their dynamic features.

S. No.	Usage Category	Task performed With ease	Task performed with difficulty	Task not performed
1.	Reading Newsgroup	22/25	02/25	01/25
2.	Link Navigation	22/25	02/25	01/25
3.	Keyword Search	15/25	07/25	03/25
4.	Making Queries	12/25	10/25	03/25
5.	Form Filling	11/25	07/25	07/25
6.	Mailing	10/25	05/25	10/25
7.	Making Transaction	01/25	01/25	19/25
8.	Social Networking	00/25	01/25	24/25

Table 7.2: User Evaluation Analysis

7.4 CONCLUSIONS

Following are the results and Innovations Claimed by this Research Work:

A. An Enhanced Web Browser WACTA is designed and developed for visually challenged users, with improved HCI features. The prototype is already tested for 25 skilled blind users and they have found it user friendly as it fulfills their basic requirements to access the internet effectively for both routine and important tasks.
B. Need for of direct speech enabled Public Utility Websites for visually challenged users is highlighted and a novel framework for the same is proposed (chapter 4).
C. A VoiceXML / VOIP based Client Interface Framework is designed for IVRS like Interactive system on Computer without the use of telephony (Chapter 5).
D. A hierarchical model for Performance Evaluation of Internet Assistive Tools in quantitative terms is proposed (Chapter 6).

CHAPTER 8
CONCLUSIONS AND FUTURE DIRECTIONS

8.1 INTRODUCTION AND WORK SUMMARY

This Research work addresses some of the important issues related to accessibility in context of visually challenged web users. First concern is the availability of an effective yet affordable speech based web browser for them. WACTA Web Browser is designed and developed to cater this need. Still, it is established that certain crucial tasks related to public utility e.g. Railways Reservation should be made speech-enabled by the site owners directly on their websites so that visually challenged users may use the facility from anywhere. The Framework designed by us for this task can speech-enable an existing site at an affordable cost and effort. We have also proposed a framework for IVRS like system on computer using VoiceXML/ VOIP which can handle domain specific complex web interactions without the need of telephone. Some work is also done by us in performance evaluation of Assistive Tools which has been relatively an untouched area.

8.2 CONTRIBUTIONS OF THE RESEARCH WORK

This research work contributes to the design, development and evaluation of a speech based web browser prototype and design frameworks for performing specific tasks by visually challenged users.

We believe that the research work done by us is an important one, which should be brought to the notice of researchers, industry and responsible public organizations. This research work is expected to make the following impacts:

- The web browser designed and developed by us shall cater the needs of visually challenged users and shall be continually enhanced and extended in future.

- The research work shall create accessibility awareness among all concerned.

- The research work shall trigger further researches and set a standard for futuristic websites where accessibility and usability rights of each individual may be ensured.

8.3 FUTURE DIRECTIONS

The solutions to accessibility problem demands co-operation and co-ordination among all concerned e.g. Website Owners, Web designers, Authoring Tools Developers, Assistive Technology Developers, Researchers, Public Terminal (Computer) Facilitators, policy Makers, Visually Challenged users etc. Awareness regarding accessibility issues may bring these parties to work in close coordination.

Assistive Technology needs continuous and concerted efforts to keep pace with the fast developments in the Web Technology. The problem is, till the time, ATs find solution to a current Web issue, an altogether new issue is already set. Traditionally, an industry criterion for making investment on a project has been determined by the number of use cases offered by the aimed product. Thus, investments on ATs may not gain due importance due to its small market size.

This research work has strengthened our belief that knowledge and technology should be used in favor of mankind to every possible extent. Internet is a wonderful tool having ability to compensate the visual impairment with its technology. Design and development of powerful yet affordable speech based interfaces would be certainly helpful in enhancing the overall Quality of Life of visually challenged.

The work done by us shall be further taken up in future e.g. enhancing the features and capabilities of WACTA web browser, its design and development for Android based Tablet Computers as well as extending it for Hindi scripted websites.

REFERENCES

[1].   Steinmetz R., and Nahrstedt K. (2004) *Multimedia Applications*, Springer.

[2].   Enabling Dimensions, access date 2002 [Internet]. Usage of Computers and Internet by the Visually Challenged: Issues and Challenges in the Indian context, *Findings of a study conducted by Enabling Dimensions*, January, 2002.

[3].   Cynthia, Shelly and George, Young (2006), *Writing Accessible Web Applications, Microsoft Accessibility Technology For Everyone*, 2006. Microsoft Press.

[4].   Practical E-Commerce, http://www.practicalecommerce.com/articles/2114-Screen-Readers-Eight-Frequently-Asked-Questions Access Date: July, 2012

[5].   Chisholm W. and Henery S., (2005),   Interdependent components of Web Accessibility, in *Proceedings of W4A at WWW2005: International Cross-Disciplinary Workshop on Web Accessibility*, ACM Press 2005

[6].   Evaluating Web Sites for Accessibility: Overview [Internet]. [updated 2009]. The World Wide Web Consortium; http://www.w3.org/WAI/eval/Overview.html

[7].   Verma P., Singh R., Singh A. K., Yadav V., Pandey A.(2010), An Enhanced Speech-based Internet Browsing System for Visually Challenged", In *ICCCT 2010*. DOI: 10.1109/ICCCT.2010.5640374

[8].   Brajnik Giorgio, Cancila Daniela, Nicoli Daniela, Pignatelli Mery (2005), Do text transcoders improve usability for disabled users?, In *W4A at WWW2005*. ACM 2005.

[9].   Web Accessibility Initiative (WAI) [Internet]. [updated 2010]. The World Wide Web Consortium (W3C); http://www.w3.org/WAI/

[10]. Web Content Accessibility Guidelines (WCAG) Overview [Internet]. [updated 2009]. The World Wide Web Consortium; [Access Date Feb 2012]. Available from: http://www.w3.org/WAI/intro/wcag.php

[11]. Authoring Tool Accessibility Guidelines (ATAG) Overview [Internet]. [updated 2008]. The World Wide Web Consortium; [Access Date Feb 2012]. Available from: http://www.w3.org/WAI/intro/atag.php

[12]. User Agent Accessibility Guidelines (UAAG) Overview [Internet]. [updated 2009]. The World Wide Web Consortium; http://www.w3.org/WAI/intro/uaag.html

[13]. WAI-ARIA Overview [Internet]. [updated 2009]. The World Wide Web Consortium; [Access Date Feb 2012]. Available from: http://www.w3.org/WAI/intro/aria.php

[14]. Freedom Scientific access date March 2012 [http://www.freedomscientific.com/] access on June, 2012.

[15]. Harper S. and Patel N., (2005) Gist summaries for visually challenged surfers, In *ASSETS'05: Proceedings of the 7th international ACM SIGCCESS conference on Computers and accessibility, pages 90-97*, 2005.

[16]. EMACSPEAK, access date March 2012. [http://emacspeak.sourceforge.net/smithsonian/study.html].

[17]. Zajicek M., Powell C., and Reeves C., (1999), Web search and orientation with Bookestalk, in *Proceedings of tech. and Persons with disabilities Conf.*, 1999.

[18]. Mahmud Jalal, Borodin Yevgen and Ramakrishnan I. V. (2007), CSurf: A Context-Driven Non-Visual Web-Browser, *In WWW2007/ Track: Browsers and User Interfaces*.2007.

[19]. Raman T. V.(1994). *Aster: Audio system for technical reading*, Ph.D. Thesis, Cornell University, 1994.

[20]. Huang and Sundaresan N., (2000), A semantic transcoding system to adapt web services for users with disabilities, *In ASSETS*, 2000.

[21]. Ramakrishnan I., Stent A., and Yang A. (2004), Hearsay: Enabling audio browsing on hypertext content. *In www, 2004*.

[22]. Media Lab Asia [http://medialabasia.in/index.php/shruti-drishti]. Access on June 2012.

[23]. National Association For the Blinds [http://www.nabdelhi.org/NAB_SAFA.htm] Access on May 2012

[24]. Browse Aloud [http://www.browsealoud.com] Access on June 2012.

[25]. Bigham J., Prince C, AND Ladner R (2008) WebAnywhere: A Screen Reader On-the-Go., *In W4A2008 -Technical, April 21-22, 2008, Beijing, China. Co-Located with the 17th International World Wide Web Conference.*

[26]. Document Object Model, [Internet]. http:// www.w3.org/DOM/[^] access date July, 2012

[27]. Bigham J., and Ladner R. (2007). Accessmonkey: A Collaborative Scripting Framework for Web Users and Developers, *In W4A2007 Technical Paper May 07–08, 2007, Banff, Canada. Co-Located with the 16th International World Wide Web Conference.*

[28]. WEBINSIGHT, accessed 2012 [http://webinsight.cs.washington.edu/accessibility/].

[29]. VoiceXML 2.0, [http://www.w3.org/TR/voicexml20/] accessed March, 2011.

[30]. VoiceXML 2.1, [http://www.w3.org/TR/voicexml21/] (accessed 26th March, 2011)

[31]. VoXML, [http://www.voxml.org/] (accessed 26th March, 2011)

[32]. Markowitz J., (1996). *Using Speech Recognition*, Prentice-Hall, NJ.

[33]. W3C: Extensible Markup Language (2004) (XML) 1.0 (Third Edition), Feb 2004. http://www.w3.org/TR/2004/REC-xml-20040204/

[34]. Montiel-Hern´andez, J. and Cuay´ahuitl, H. (2004), SUIML: A Markup Language for Facilitating Automatic Speech Application Development, *In proceedings of theMICAI'04 (WIC), Mexico City, Mexico, Apr 2004.*

[35]. Heriberto Cuay´ahuitl, Miguel ´Angel Rodr´ıguez-Moreno, and Juventino Montiel-Hern´andez (2004), VoiceBuilder: A Framework for Automatic Speech Application Development, *In INTERSPEECH 2004.*

[36]. Chauhan Himanshu, Dhoolia Pankaj, Nambiar Ullas , Verma Ashish (2006), WAV: Voice Access to Web Information for Masses, *In 22nd International Conference on Data Engineering (ICDE) April 3-8, Atlanta, 2006.*

[37]. Bigham J. P., Lau T. A. and Nichols J. W. (2009), TrailBlazer: Enabling Blind Users to Blaze Trails Through the Web, *In International Conference on Intelligent User Interfaces, Florida, 2009.*

[38]. Stanislav Ondáš and Jozef Juhár (2010), "Development and Evaluation of the Spoken Dialogue System Based on the W3C Recommendations", Products and Services; from R&D to Final Solutions, DOI: 10.5772/297, ISBN: 978-953-307-211-1.

[39]. Paraiso E. C., and Barthes J. P. A (2005), An Intelligent Speech Interface for Personal Assistants in R&D Projects. *In CSCWD 2005 - The 9th IEEE International Conference on CSCW in Design, Coventry - UK, v. 2. pp. 804-809, 2005.*

[40]. Paraiso E. C., Campbell Yuri, Tacla Cesar A. (2008), WebAnima: A Web-Based Embodied Conversational Assistant to Interface Users with Multi-Agent-Based CSCW Applications, 337-342. *In CSCWD2008.*

[41]. Jordi Luque, Daniel Ferrés, Javier Hernando, José B. Mariño and Horacio Rodríguez. (2006), GeoVAQA: A Voice Activated Geographical Question Answering System. *Actas de las IV Jornadas en Tecnología del Habla (4JTH). Zaragoza, Spain,* November 2006.

[42]. Wang Hsin-min, Chen Berlin, Shen Liang-jui, and Chang Chao chi (2001), A Voice-Activated Web-based Mandarin Chinese Spoken Document Retrieval System, *In ICCPOL2001.*

[43]. Fabbrizio Giuseppe Di, Lewis Charles (2004). Florence: a Dialogue Manager Framework for Spoken Dialogue Systems, *In ICSLP 2004, 8th International Conference on Spoken Language Processing, Jeju, Jeju Island, Korea, October 4-8, 2004.*

[44]. Daly J., Forgue M., Hirakawa (2008), World Wide Web Consortium Issues VoiceXML 2.0 and Speech Recognition Grammar as W3C Recommendations, available online at: http://www.w3.org/2004/03/voicexml2-pressrelease (accessed 26th March, 2008).

[45]. Bansiya J. and Davis C.G. (2002), A Hierarchical Model for Object-Oriented Design Quality Assessment, IEEE Trans. Software Eng., vol. 28, no. 1, pp. 4-17, January 2002.

[46]. Lazar Jonathan, Allen Aaron, Kleinman Jason and Malarkey Chris (2007), What Frustrates Screen Reader Users on the Web: A Study of 100 Blind Users, International Journal of Human-Computer Interaction, 22:3, 247-269. 2007.

[47]. Bigham Jeffrey P., Cavender Anna C., Brudvik Jeremy T., Wobbrock Jacob O. and Ladner Richard E. (2007), WebinSitu: A Comparative Analysis of Blind and Sighted Browsing Behavior, *In ASSETS'07, October 15-17, 2007.*

[48]. Sloan David, Heath Andy, Hamilton Fraser, Kelly Brian, Petrie Helen, Phipps Lawrie (2006), Contextual Web Accessibility – Maximizing the benefits of Accessibility Guidelines, In *W4A at WWW2006. ACM 2006.*

[49]. Cooper Michael (2007), Accessibility of Emerging Rich Web Technologies: Web 2.0 and the Semantic Web, *In W4A2007- Keynote, 2007.*

[50]. Leporini Barbara and Paterno Fabio, Applying Web Usability Criteria for Vision-Challenged Users: Does It Really Improve Task Performance?, International Journal of Human-Computer Interaction, 24:1, 17-47. 2008.

APPENDIX - I
CODE FOR WACTA WEB BROWSER

Form1.cs

```
using System;
using System.Windows;
using System.Windows.Forms;
using System.Speech.Synthesis;
using System.Windows.Input;


namespace Browser
{
    public partial class Form1 : Form
    {
        int i;
        int k;
        Boolean pausestate;
        HtmlElement x;
        HtmlElement el;
        int count;
        HtmlElementCollection htmCollect;
        SpeechSynthesizer syn = new SpeechSynthesizer();

        public Form1()
        {
            InitializeComponent();
            this.KeyPreview = true;
            this.Focus();
            this.textBox1.Focus();
            syn.SpeakAsync("Web Browser Wactaa initialized. Please press alt + L to Enter the
address");

        }

        private void webBrowser1_DocumentTitleChanged(object sender, EventArgs e)
        {
            this.Text = webBrowser1.DocumentTitle.ToString();

        }

        private void textBox1_KeyDown(object sender, System.Windows.Forms.KeyEventArgs e)
        {

            syn.SpeakAsync((e.KeyData).ToString());
```

```
   if (e.KeyValue == (char)13)
   {
       i = 0;
       k = 0;
       pausestate = false;
       webBrowser1.Navigate(textBox1.Text);

   }
}


private void webBrowser1_Navigated(object sender,
   WebBrowserNavigatedEventArgs e)                .
{
   webBrowser1.Dispose();

}

private void Form1_Load(object sender, EventArgs e)
{
   buttonBack.Enabled = false;
   buttonForward.Enabled = false;
   buttonStop.Enabled = false;

   this.textBox1.Focus();
}

private void buttonBack_Click(object sender, EventArgs e)
{
   syn.SpeakAsync("Back");
   i = 0;
   k = 0;
   htmCollect = null;
   webBrowser1.GoBack();
   textBox1.Text = webBrowser1.Url.ToString();
}


private void buttonForward_Click(object sender, EventArgs e)
{
   syn.SpeakAsync("Forward");
   i = 0;
   k = 0;
   htmCollect = null;
   webBrowser1.GoForward();
   textBox1.Text = webBrowser1.Url.ToString();
}



private void buttonStop_Click(object sender, EventArgs e)
```

```
{
    syn.SpeakAsync("Stop");
    webBrowser1.Stop();
}

private void buttonHome_Click(object sender, EventArgs e)
{
    syn.SpeakAsync("Home");
    i = 0;
    k = 0;
    htmCollect = null;
    webBrowser1.GoHome();

}

private void buttonRefresh_Click(object sender, EventArgs e)
{
    syn.SpeakAsync("Refresh");
    webBrowser1.Refresh();
    i = 0;
    k = 0;
    htmCollect = null;
}

private void buttonSubmit_Click(object sender, EventArgs e)
{
    syn.SpeakAsync("Go");
    Navigate(textBox1.Text);

}

// Navigates to the given URL if it is valid.
private void Navigate(String address)
{
    i = 0;
    k = 0;
    htmCollect = null;
    pausestate = false;
    syn.SpeakAsyncCancelAll();
    if (String.IsNullOrEmpty(address)) return;
    if (address.Equals("about:blank")) return;
    if (!address.StartsWith("http://") &&
        !address.StartsWith("https://"))
    {
        address = "http://" + address;
    }
    try
    {
        webBrowser1.AllowNavigation = true;
        webBrowser1.Navigate(new Uri(address));
    }

    catch (System.UriFormatException)
```

```
        {
            return;
        }
    }

    private void webBrowser1_CanGoBackChanged(object sender, EventArgs e)
    {
        if (webBrowser1.CanGoBack == true)
        {
            buttonBack.Enabled = true;
        }
        else
        {
            buttonBack.Enabled = false;
        }
    }

    private void webBrowser1_CanGoForwardChanged(object sender, EventArgs e)
    {
        if (webBrowser1.CanGoForward == true)
        {
            buttonForward.Enabled = true;
        }
        else
        {
            buttonForward.Enabled = false;
        }
    }

    private void webBrowser1_Navigating(object sender,
        WebBrowserNavigatingEventArgs e)
    {
        buttonStop.Enabled = true;


    }


    private void webBrowser1_DocumentCompleted(object sender,
WebBrowserDocumentCompletedEventArgs e)
    {
        i = 0;
        k = 0;
        htmCollect = null;
        pausestate = false;
        webBrowser1.PreviewKeyDown -= new
PreviewKeyDownEventHandler(webBrowser1_PreviewKeyDown);
        textBox1.Text = webBrowser1.Url.ToString();
        if (webBrowser1.Document != null)
        {
            el = webBrowser1.Document.Body;
            htmCollect = el.All;
            count = htmCollect.Count;
```

```csharp
// webBrowser1.AllowNavigation = true;
webBrowser1.ScriptErrorsSuppressed = true;
syn.SpeakAsync("The page is loaded");
webBrowser1.Document.Focus();
syn.SpeakAsync("Title of this webpage is");
syn.SpeakAsync(webBrowser1.DocumentTitle);
buttonStop.Enabled = false;
webBrowser1.Document.ContextMenuShowing += new
HtmlElementEventHandler(Document_ContextMenuShowing);
webBrowser1.Document.ActiveElement.Focusing += new
HtmlElementEventHandler(ActiveElement_Focusing);
webBrowser1.Document.ActiveElement.LosingFocus += new
HtmlElementEventHandler(ActiveElement_LosingFocus);
webBrowser1.PreviewKeyDown += new
PreviewKeyDownEventHandler(webBrowser1_PreviewKeyDown);
webBrowser1.Document.ActiveElement.KeyDown += new
HtmlElementEventHandler(ActiveElement_KeyDown);

        this.KeyDown += new
System.Windows.Forms.KeyEventHandler(this.Form1_KeyDown);

    }
}

    void webBrowser1_PreviewKeyDown(object sender, PreviewKeyDownEventArgs e)
    {

        if (e.KeyCode == Keys.Down)
        {
           x = htmCollect[i];
           x.Enabled = true;

           if (x.TagName.ToLower() == "img")
           {
              syn.SpeakAsync("Image");
              syn.SpeakAsync(x.GetAttribute("alt"));
              if (i < count - 1)
                 i++;

              x = htmCollect[i];
              return;
           }


        if (x.TagName.ToString().ToLower() == "input" || x.ToString().ToLower() == "select"
|| x.TagName.ToString().ToLower() == "option" || x.TagName.ToString().ToLower() ==
"textarea")
           {

              if (x.GetAttribute("type").ToString().ToLower() == "submit")
              {
```

```
        syn.SpeakAsync("Submit");
        x.Focus();
    }

    if (x.GetAttribute("type").ToString().ToLower()== "text")
    {
        syn.SpeakAsync("textbox");

    }

    syn.SpeakAsync(x.TagName);

    x.Focus();
    if (i < count - 1)
        i++;

    x = htmCollect[i];
    return;
}


while (x.InnerText == null)
{
    if (i < count - 1)
        i++;

    x = htmCollect[i];
}


String str1 = x.InnerText;

String str2 = x.InnerHtml;

String str3;


while (!(str1.Equals(str2)))
{
    int j = 0;
    while (j < str1.Length && str1[j] == str2[j])
    {
        j++;
    }
    str3 = str1.Substring(0, j);

    if (str3 != null)
    {
        x.Focus();
        syn.SpeakAsync(str3);
        x.ScrollIntoView(true);
```

```
        if (i < count - 1)
           i++;

        x = htmCollect[i];
     }
     while (x.InnerText == null)
     {
        if (i < count - 1)
           i++;

        x = htmCollect[i];
     }

     str1 = x.InnerText;

     str2 = x.InnerHtml;

  }

  if (str1.Equals(str2))
  {
     if (x.TagName.ToLower() == "a" && x.InnerText != null)
     {

        x.Focus();
        syn.SpeakAsync(x.InnerText.ToString());
        x.ScrollIntoView(true);
        if (i < count - 1)
           i++;

        x = htmCollect[i];
        return;
     }

     if (x.InnerText != null)
     {
        syn.SpeakAsync(x.InnerText.ToString());
        x.ScrollIntoView(true);
     }

     if (i < count - 1)
        i++;

     x = htmCollect[i];
     return;
  }

}
```

```
// Up Key Press

if (e.KeyCode == Keys.Up)
{

 x = htmCollect[i];

while (x.InnerText == null)
{
   if (i > 0)
      i--;

   x = htmCollect[i];
}


String str1 = x.InnerText;

String str2 = x.InnerHtml;

String str3;


while (!(str1.Equals(str2)))
{

   int j = 0;
   while (j < str1.Length && str1[j] == str2[j])
   {
      j++;
   }
   str3 = str1.Substring(0, j);

   if (str3 != null)
   {
      x.Focus();
      syn.SpeakAsync(str3);
      x.ScrollIntoView(true);
   }

   if (i > 0)
      i--;

   x = htmCollect[i];
   while (x.InnerText == null)
   {
      if (i > 0)
      i--;

   x = htmCollect[i];
   }
```

```csharp
            str1 = x.InnerText;

            str2 = x.InnerHtml;

        }


        if (str1.Equals(str2))
        {
            if (x.TagName.ToLower() == "a" && x.InnerText != null)
            {
                x.Focus();
                //syn.SpeakAsync(x.InnerText.ToString());
                x.ScrollIntoView(true);
                if (i > 0)
                i--;

            x = htmCollect[i];
                return;
            }

            if (x.InnerText !=null)
                syn.SpeakAsync(x.InnerText.ToString());
                x.ScrollIntoView(true);


        if (i > 0)
            i--;

        x = htmCollect[i];
            return;


        }

        }


        if (e.KeyCode == Keys.Left)
        {
            if (syn != null && syn.Rate > -10)
                syn.Rate--;

        }

        if (e.KeyCode == Keys.Right)
        {
            if (syn != null && syn.Rate < 10)
                syn.Rate++;

        }
        if (e.KeyCode == Keys.Escape)
        {
```

```csharp
        syn.SpeakAsyncCancelAll();


        }

        if (e.KeyCode == Keys.ControlKey)
        {
            if (!pausestate)
            {
                syn.Pause();
                pausestate = true;
                return;
            }
            else
            {

                syn.Resume();
                pausestate = false;
                return;
            }

        }



    }


    private void Form1_KeyDown(object sender, System.Windows.Forms.KeyEventArgs e)
    {

        if (e.Alt && e.KeyCode == Keys.L)
        {
            this.textBox1.Focus();
            textBox1.Clear();
            e.Handled = true;
            syn.SpeakAsync("Address Bar");
        }
    }


    void ActiveElement_Focusing(object sender, HtmlElementEventArgs e)
    {
        //int j = 0;
        HtmlElement tb;
        tb = webBrowser1.Document.ActiveElement;
        if (webBrowser1.Document != null && tb.TagName != "body" &&
webBrowser1.Document.ActiveElement != null)
        {

            if (tb.TagName.ToString().ToLower() == "a")
```

94

```
        {
           syn.SpeakAsync("Link");
           syn.SpeakAsync(tb.InnerText.ToString());
        }
        //syn.Speak(elem.Name.ToString());

        if (tb.TagName.ToString().ToLower() == "textarea")
        {
           syn.SpeakAsync("textarea");
        }
        if (tb.TagName.ToString().ToLower() == "input")
        {
           syn.SpeakAsync(tb.GetAttribute("type"));
        }

        if (tb.TagName.ToString().ToLower() == "select" || tb.TagName.ToString().ToLower()
== "option")
        {

           foreach (HtmlElement ch in tb.Children)
           {
              ch.Focus();
              syn.SpeakAsync(ch.InnerText.ToString());
              Console.Read();
           }
        }

     }


}

void ActiveElement_LosingFocus(object sender, HtmlElementEventArgs e)
{
   syn.SpeakAsyncCancelAll();
}


void ActiveElement_KeyDown(Object sender, HtmlElementEventArgs e)
{
   int i = e.KeyPressedCode;
   char c = (char)i;
   syn.SpeakAsync(c.ToString());
   e.BubbleEvent = false;

}


private void Form1_Load_1(object sender, EventArgs e)
{

}
```

```csharp
private void buttonMouse_Click(object sender, EventArgs e)
{

    // syn.Speak("Right Click the mouse at some point of webpage to get the glimpse of text
underneath it");
}

private void buttonNews_Click(object sender, EventArgs e)
{

    HtmlElement el = webBrowser1.Document.Body;
    el.Focus();
    HtmlElement el1;
    el1 = webBrowser1.Document.ActiveElement;
    if (el1 != null && el1.InnerText != null)
    {

        syn.SpeakAsync((el1.InnerText).ToString());

    }


}

private void buttonInteract_Click(object sender, EventArgs e)
{
    // Step I:  Speak the Title of the Document
    syn.SpeakAsync("Title of this webpage is");
    syn.SpeakAsync(webBrowser1.DocumentTitle);
    // Step I:  Speak the Domain of the Document for security purpose
    syn.SpeakAsync("Domain of this webpage is");
    syn.Speak(webBrowser1.Document.Domain);
    // Step II: Speak the Background colorof the webpage
    syn.SpeakAsync("Background Color of this webpage is set to");
    syn.SpeakAsync(webBrowser1.Document.BackColor.ToString());
    // Step III: Speak the <H1> Elements of the webpage
    HtmlElementCollection theElementCollection1;
    theElementCollection1 = webBrowser1.Document.GetElementsByTagName("H1");
    syn.SpeakAsync("These are the Headings of the webpage");
    foreach (HtmlElement curElement in theElementCollection1)
    {

        if (curElement.InnerText != null)
        {
            syn.SpeakAsync((curElement.InnerText.ToString()));

        }

    }
    syn.SpeakAsync("Number of Links on this web page are");
    syn.SpeakAsync(webBrowser1.Document.Links.Count.ToString());
```

```
            }

        private void Document_ContextMenuShowing(Object sender, HtmlElementEventArgs e)
        {
            if (webBrowser1.Document != null)
            {
                HtmlElement elem =
webBrowser1.Document.GetElementFromPoint(e.ClientMousePosition);
                if (elem != null && elem.TagName.ToLower() !="body" && elem.InnerText != null)
                {

                    //syn.SpeakAsync(elem.InnerText.ToString());
                    elem.Focus();
                    return;
                }
            }
        }

        private void buttonQuery_Click(object sender, EventArgs e)
        {

            textBox2.Focus();
            textBox2.Clear();
            syn.Speak("Enter the text you want to search on this website and press escape");


        }


        private void textBox2_KeyDown(object sender, System.Windows.Forms.KeyEventArgs e)
        {

            syn.SpeakAsync((e.KeyData).ToString());
            HtmlDocument doc = webBrowser1.Document;


            if (e.KeyValue == (char)13)
            {
                String srch;
                String str;
                String url = doc.Url.ToString();
                srch = textBox2.Text;
                str = "www.google.com/search?q=" + srch + "&sitesearch=" + url;
                if (!str.StartsWith("http://") &&
                !str.StartsWith("https://"))
                {
                    str = "http://" + str;
                }

                webBrowser1.Navigate(str);
                textBox1.Text = str;
            }
        }
```

```csharp
        private void textBox2_TextChanged(object sender, EventArgs e)
        {

        }

        private void textBox1_TextChanged(object sender, EventArgs e)
        {

        }

    }
}
```

//Browser.Program

Program.cs

```csharp
using System;
using System.Collections.Generic;
using System.Windows.Forms;
using System.Speech.Synthesis;

namespace Browser
{
    static class Program
    {
        /// <summary>
        /// The main entry point for the application.
        /// </summary>
        [STAThread]
        static void Main()
        {
            Application.EnableVisualStyles();
            Application.SetCompatibleTextRenderingDefault(false);
            Application.Run(new Form1());
        }
    }
}
```

Form1.Designer.cs

```csharp
namespace Browser
{
    partial class Form1
    {
        /// <summary>
        /// Required designer variable.
        /// </summary>
        private System.ComponentModel.IContainer components = null;

        /// <summary>
```

```
            /// Clean up any resources being used.
            /// </summary>
            /// <param name="disposing">true if managed resources should be disposed;
otherwise, false.</param>
            protected override void Dispose(bool disposing)
            {
                if (disposing && (components != null))
                {
                    components.Dispose();
                }
                base.Dispose(disposing);
            }

            #region Windows Form Designer generated code

            /// <summary>
            /// Required method for Designer support - do not modify
            /// the contents of this method with the code editor.
            /// </summary>
            private void InitializeComponent()
            {
                this.webBrowser1 = new System.Windows.Forms.WebBrowser();
                this.textBox1 = new System.Windows.Forms.TextBox();
                this.buttonSubmit = new System.Windows.Forms.Button();
                this.buttonRefresh = new System.Windows.Forms.Button();
                this.buttonHome = new System.Windows.Forms.Button();
                this.buttonStop = new System.Windows.Forms.Button();
                this.buttonForward = new System.Windows.Forms.Button();
                this.buttonBack = new System.Windows.Forms.Button();
                this.buttonNews = new System.Windows.Forms.Button();
                this.buttonMouse = new System.Windows.Forms.Button();
                this.buttonInteract = new System.Windows.Forms.Button();
                this.buttonQuery = new System.Windows.Forms.Button();
                this.textBox2 = new System.Windows.Forms.TextBox();
                this.SuspendLayout();
                //
                // webBrowser1
                //
                this.webBrowser1.Anchor =
((System.Windows.Forms.AnchorStyles)(((((System.Windows.Forms.AnchorStyles.Top |
System.Windows.Forms.AnchorStyles.Bottom)
                            | System.Windows.Forms.AnchorStyles.Left)
                            | System.Windows.Forms.AnchorStyles.Right)));
                this.webBrowser1.Location = new System.Drawing.Point(1, 73);
                this.webBrowser1.MinimumSize = new System.Drawing.Size(20, 20);
                this.webBrowser1.Name = "webBrowser1";
                this.webBrowser1.Size = new System.Drawing.Size(986, 456);
                this.webBrowser1.TabIndex = 15;
                this.webBrowser1.DocumentCompleted += new
System.Windows.Forms.WebBrowserDocumentCompletedEventHandler(this.webBrowser1_Docu
mentCompleted);
                //
                // textBox1
                //
                this.textBox1.Location = new System.Drawing.Point(14, 47);
                this.textBox1.Name = "textBox1";
                this.textBox1.Size = new System.Drawing.Size(727, 20);
                this.textBox1.TabIndex = 14;
                this.textBox1.TextChanged += new
System.EventHandler(this.textBox1_TextChanged);
```

```
            this.textBox1.KeyDown += new
System.Windows.Forms.KeyEventHandler(this.textBox1_KeyDown);
            //
            // buttonSubmit
            //
            this.buttonSubmit.Location = new System.Drawing.Point(762, 18);
            this.buttonSubmit.Name = "buttonSubmit";
            this.buttonSubmit.Size = new System.Drawing.Size(75, 49);
            this.buttonSubmit.TabIndex = 13;
            this.buttonSubmit.Text = "&Go";
            this.buttonSubmit.UseVisualStyleBackColor = true;
            this.buttonSubmit.Click += new
System.EventHandler(this.buttonSubmit_Click);
            //
            // buttonRefresh
            //
            this.buttonRefresh.Location = new System.Drawing.Point(302, 18);
            this.buttonRefresh.Name = "buttonRefresh";
            this.buttonRefresh.Size = new System.Drawing.Size(68, 23);
            this.buttonRefresh.TabIndex = 12;
            this.buttonRefresh.Text = "&Refresh";
            this.buttonRefresh.UseVisualStyleBackColor = true;
            this.buttonRefresh.Click += new
System.EventHandler(this.buttonRefresh_Click);
            //
            // buttonHome
            //
            this.buttonHome.Location = new System.Drawing.Point(229, 18);
            this.buttonHome.Name = "buttonHome";
            this.buttonHome.Size = new System.Drawing.Size(67, 23);
            this.buttonHome.TabIndex = 11;
            this.buttonHome.Text = "&Home";
            this.buttonHome.UseVisualStyleBackColor = true;
            this.buttonHome.Click += new
System.EventHandler(this.buttonHome_Click);
            //
            // buttonStop
            //
            this.buttonStop.Location = new System.Drawing.Point(159, 18);
            this.buttonStop.Name = "buttonStop";
            this.buttonStop.Size = new System.Drawing.Size(64, 23);
            this.buttonStop.TabIndex = 10;
            this.buttonStop.Text = "&Stop";
            this.buttonStop.UseVisualStyleBackColor = true;
            this.buttonStop.Click += new
System.EventHandler(this.buttonStop_Click);
            //
            // buttonForward
            //
            this.buttonForward.Location = new System.Drawing.Point(87, 18);
            this.buttonForward.Name = "buttonForward";
            this.buttonForward.Size = new System.Drawing.Size(66, 23);
            this.buttonForward.TabIndex = 9;
            this.buttonForward.Text = "&Forward";
            this.buttonForward.UseVisualStyleBackColor = true;
            this.buttonForward.Click += new
System.EventHandler(this.buttonForward_Click);
            //
            // buttonBack
            //
```

```
            this.buttonBack.Location = new System.Drawing.Point(14, 18);
            this.buttonBack.Name = "buttonBack";
            this.buttonBack.Size = new System.Drawing.Size(67, 23);
            this.buttonBack.TabIndex = 8;
            this.buttonBack.Text = "&Back";
            this.buttonBack.UseVisualStyleBackColor = true;
            this.buttonBack.Click += new
System.EventHandler(this.buttonBack_Click);
            //
            // buttonNews
            //
            this.buttonNews.Location = new System.Drawing.Point(376, 18);
            this.buttonNews.Name = "buttonNews";
            this.buttonNews.Size = new System.Drawing.Size(75, 23);
            this.buttonNews.TabIndex = 16;
            this.buttonNews.Text = "&News_style";
            this.buttonNews.UseVisualStyleBackColor = true;
            this.buttonNews.Click += new
System.EventHandler(this.buttonNews_Click);
            //
            // buttonMouse
            //
            this.buttonMouse.Location = new System.Drawing.Point(457, 18);
            this.buttonMouse.Name = "buttonMouse";
            this.buttonMouse.Size = new System.Drawing.Size(85, 23);
            this.buttonMouse.TabIndex = 17;
            this.buttonMouse.Text = "&MouseGlimpse";
            this.buttonMouse.UseVisualStyleBackColor = true;
            this.buttonMouse.Click += new
System.EventHandler(this.buttonMouse_Click);
            //
            // buttonInteract
            //
            this.buttonInteract.Location = new System.Drawing.Point(548, 18);
            this.buttonInteract.Name = "buttonInteract";
            this.buttonInteract.Size = new System.Drawing.Size(75, 23);
            this.buttonInteract.TabIndex = 18;
            this.buttonInteract.Text = "&Interact";
            this.buttonInteract.UseVisualStyleBackColor = true;
            this.buttonInteract.Click += new
System.EventHandler(this.buttonInteract_Click);
            //
            // buttonQuery
            //
            this.buttonQuery.Location = new System.Drawing.Point(629, 18);
            this.buttonQuery.Name = "buttonQuery";
            this.buttonQuery.Size = new System.Drawing.Size(85, 23);
            this.buttonQuery.TabIndex = 19;
            this.buttonQuery.Text = "&Query";
            this.buttonQuery.UseVisualStyleBackColor = true;
            this.buttonQuery.Click += new
System.EventHandler(this.buttonQuery_Click);
            //
            // textBox2
            //
            this.textBox2.Location = new System.Drawing.Point(87, 653);
            this.textBox2.Name = "textBox2";
            this.textBox2.Size = new System.Drawing.Size(727, 20);
            this.textBox2.TabIndex = 20;
```

```
            this.textBox2.TextChanged += new
System.EventHandler(this.textBox2_TextChanged);
            this.textBox2.KeyDown += new
System.Windows.Forms.KeyEventHandler(this.textBox2_KeyDown);
            //
            // Form1
            //
            this.AccessibleDescription = "Wacta the speech based web browser for
visually impaired";
            this.AccessibleName = "wacta";
            this.AutoScaleDimensions = new System.Drawing.SizeF(6F, 13F);
            this.AutoScaleMode = System.Windows.Forms.AutoScaleMode.Font;
            this.ClientSize = new System.Drawing.Size(999, 530);
            this.Controls.Add(this.textBox2);
            this.Controls.Add(this.buttonQuery);
            this.Controls.Add(this.buttonInteract);
            this.Controls.Add(this.buttonMouse);
            this.Controls.Add(this.buttonNews);
            this.Controls.Add(this.webBrowser1);
            this.Controls.Add(this.textBox1);
            this.Controls.Add(this.buttonSubmit);
            this.Controls.Add(this.buttonRefresh);
            this.Controls.Add(this.buttonHome);
            this.Controls.Add(this.buttonStop);
            this.Controls.Add(this.buttonForward);
            this.Controls.Add(this.buttonBack);
            this.ForeColor = System.Drawing.Color.Black;
            this.Name = "Form1";
            this.Text = "WACTA";
            this.Load += new System.EventHandler(this.Form1_Load_1);
            this.KeyDown += new
System.Windows.Forms.KeyEventHandler(this.Form1_KeyDown);
            this.ResumeLayout(false);
            this.PerformLayout();

        }

        #endregion

        private System.Windows.Forms.WebBrowser webBrowser1;
        private System.Windows.Forms.TextBox textBox1;
        private System.Windows.Forms.Button buttonSubmit;
        private System.Windows.Forms.Button buttonRefresh;
        private System.Windows.Forms.Button buttonHome;
        private System.Windows.Forms.Button buttonStop;
        private System.Windows.Forms.Button buttonForward;
        private System.Windows.Forms.Button buttonBack;
        private System.Windows.Forms.Button buttonNews;
        private System.Windows.Forms.Button buttonMouse;
        private System.Windows.Forms.Button buttonInteract;
        private System.Windows.Forms.Button buttonQuery;
        private System.Windows.Forms.TextBox textBox2;
    }
}
```

BIBLIOGRAPHY

(i) JOURNALS AND CONFERENCES

Asakawa C. and Itoh T.(1998), User interface of a home page reader. *In ASSETS, 1998.*

Bansiya J. and Davis C.G.(2002), A Hierarchical Model for Object-Oriented Design Quality Assessment, IEEE Trans. Software Eng., vol. 28, no. 1, pp. 4-17, January 2002.

Bigham J. P., Lau T. A. and Nichols J. W.(2009), TrailBlazer: Enabling Blind Users to Blaze Trails Through the Web, submitted to *International Conference on Intelligent User Interfaces, Florida,2009.*

Bigham J., and Ladner R.(2007). Accessmonkey: A Collaborative Scripting Framework for Web Users and Developers, *in W4A2007 Technical Paper May 07–08, 2007, Banff, Canada. Co-Located with the 16th International World Wide Web Conference.*

Bigham J., Prince C, AND Ladner R (2008) WebAnywhere: A Screen Reader On-the-Go., *In W4A2008 -Technical, April 21-22, 2008, Beijing, China. Co-Located with the 17th International World Wide Web Conference.*

Bigham Jeffery P., Kaminsky Ryan S., Ladner Richard E., Oscar M. Danielsson, Gordon L. Hempten (2006) WebInSight: Making Web images accessible, In *Assets '06, USA.*

Bigham Jeffrey P., Cavender Anna C., Brudvik Jeremy T., Wobbrock Jacob O. and Ladner Richard E.(2007), WebinSitu: A Comparative Analysis of Blind and Sighted Browsing Behavior, *In ASSETS'07, October 15-17, 2007.*

Brajnik Giorgio, Cancila Daniela, Nicoli Daniela, Pignatelli Mery(2005), Do text transcoders improve usability for disabled users?, *In W4A at WWW2005.* ACM 2005.

Brkic Marija, and Matetic Maja, VoiceXML for Slavic Languages Application Development(2008), In HIS 2008, Poland. © IEEE 2008.

Chauhan Himanshu, Dhoolia Pankaj, Nambiar Ullas , Verma Ashish(2006), WAV: Voice Access to Web Information for Masses, In *22nd International Conference on Data Engineering (ICDE) April 3-8, Atlanta, 2006.*

Chisholm W. and Henery S., (2005), Interdependent components of Web Accessibility, *in Proceedings of W4A at WWW2005: International Cross-Disciplinary Workshop on Web Accessibility* ACM Press 2005

Cooper Michael(2007), Accessibility of Emerging Rich Web Technologies: Web 2.0 and the Semantic Web, *W4A2007- Keynote,* 2007.

103

Daly J., Forgue M., Hirakawa(2008), World Wide Web Consortium Issues VoiceXML 2.0 and Speech Recognition Grammar as W3C Recommendations, available online at: http://www.w3.org/2004/03/voicexml2-pressrelease (accessed 26th March, 2008).

Fabbrizio Giuseppe Di, Lewis Charles(2004). Florence: a Dialogue Manager Framework for Spoken Dialogue Systems. *ICSLP 2004, 8th International Conference on Spoken Language Processing, Jeju, Jeju Island, Korea, October 4-8, 2004.*

Fayzrakhmanov Ruslan, Gobel Max, Holzinger Wolfgang, Krupl Bernhard, Mager Andreas (2010), Modelling Web Navigation with the User in Mind, *W4A2010.* Apr 26-27, 2010, Raleigh, USA.

Ghose Ritwika, Dasgupta Tirthankar, and Basu Anupam (2010), Architecture of A Web Browser for Visually Handicapped People, 978-1-4244-5974-2/10 © IEEE.

Goose Stuart, Newman Mike, Schmidt Claus and Hue Laurent (2000), Enhancing Web accessibility via Vox Portal and a Web-hosted dynamic HTML – VoxML converter, Computer Networks 33 (2000) 583-592. Elsevier Science.

Harper S. and Patel N.,(2005) Gist summaries for visually challenged surfers, *In ASSETS'05: Proceedings of the 7th international ACM SIGCCESS conference on Computers and accessibility, pages 90-97, 2005.*

Heriberto Cuay´ahuitl, Miguel ´Angel Rodr´ıguez-Moreno, and Juventino Montiel-Hern´andez(2004), VoiceBuilder: A Framework for Automatic Speech Application Development in *INTERSPEECH 2004.*

Hori M., Kondoh G., Ono K., Hirose S. Ichi, and Singhal S.: Annotation-based web content transcoding, *In WWW, 2000.*

Huang and Sundaresan N.,(2000), A semantic transcoding system to adapt web services for users with disabilities, *In ASSETS, 2000.*

Jordi Luque, Daniel Ferrés, Javier Hernando, José B. Mariño and Horacio Rodríguez.(2006), GeoVAQA: A Voice Activated Geographical Question Answering System. Actas de las IV Jornadas en Tecnología del Habla (4JTH). Zaragoza, Spain, November 2006.

Kane Shaun K., Shulman Jessie A., Shockley Timothy J., and Ladner Richard E.(2007), A Web Accessibility Report Card for Top International University Web Sites, *In W4A2007 Communications Papers.* © 2007 ACM.

Knutsson Bjorn and Lu Honghui (2003), Architecture and Performance of Server-Directed Transcoding, ACM Transaction on Internet Technology, Vol. 3, No. 4, Nov 2003 Pages 392-424.

Lau Raymond, Flammia Giovanni, Pao Christine, and Zue Victor (1997), webGLAXY: beyond point and click- a conventional interface to a browser, Computer Networks and ISDN Systems 29 (1977) 1385 – 1393.

Lazar Jonathan, Allen Aaron, Kleinman Jason and Malarkey Chris(2007), What Frustrates Screen Reader Users on the Web: A Study of 100 Blind Users, International Journal of Human-Computer Interaction, 22:3, 247-269. 2007.

Leporini Barbara and Paterno Fabio, Applying Web Usability Criteria for Vision-Challenged Users: Does It Really Improve Task Performance?, in International Journal of Human-Computer Interaction, 24:1, 17-47. 2008.

Mahmud Jalal, Borodin Yevgen and Ramakrishnan I. V., CSurf: A Context-Driven Non-Visual Web-Browser, WWW2007/ Track: Browsers and User Interfaces.

Montiel-Hern´andez, J. and Cuay´ahuitl, H.(2004), SUIML: A Markup Language for Facilitating Automatic Speech Application Development, in *proceedings of theMICAI'04 (WIC), Mexico City, Mexico, Apr 2004.*

Muhammad Malik, Pattal Imran, Yuan LI, and Jianqiu Zeng(2009), Web 3.0: A Real Personal Web!, In *2009 Third International Conference on Next Generation Mobile Applications, Services and Technologies,* © 2009 IEEE.

Mukherjee Saikat, Ramakrishnan I.V. and Kifer Michael, Semantic Bookmarking for Non-Visual Web Access. *In ASSET'04.* © 2004 ACM.

Narayanaswami AVassiliadis Costas (2001), An Online Speech- Enabled Information Access Tool using Java Speech Application Programming Interface. 0-7803-6661-1/01, 2001. © IEEE

Paraiso E. C., and Barthes J. P. A (2005)., An Intelligent Speech Interface for Personal Assistants in R&D Projects. In: *CSCWD 2005 - The 9th IEEE International Conference on CSCW in Design, Coventry - UK,* v. 2. pp. 804-809, 2005.

Paraiso E. C., Campbell Yuri, Tacla Cesar A.(2008), WebAnima: A Web-Based Embodied Conversational Assistant to Interface Users with Multi-Agent-Based CSCW Applications, 337-342. *In CSCWD2008.*

Petrie Helen, Hamilton Fraser and King Neil (2004), Tension, what tension? Website accessibility and visual design, In W4A at WWW2004.

Pingali Prasad, Jagarlamudi Jagadeeshand Varma Vasudeva (2006), WebKhoj:vIndian language IR from Multiple Character Encoding, *In WWW2006, May23-26,2006, Edinburgh, Scotland.* © 2006 ACM.

Ramakrishnan I., Stent A., and Yang A. (2004), Hearsay: Enabling audio browsing on hypertext content. *In www, 2004.*

Raman T. V.(1994). Aster: Audio system for technical reading, Ph.D. Thesis, Cornell University, 1994.

Rollins Sami, Sundaresan Neel.(2000), AVoN calling: AXL for voice-enabled Web navigation, Computer Networks 33 (2000) 533-551. © 2000, Elsevier.

Rotard Martin, Knodler Sven, and Ertl Thomas (2005), A Tactile Web Browser for the Visually Disabled, In HT'05, Salzburg, Australia. © 2005 ACM.

Sloan David, Heath Andy, Hamilton Fraser, Kelly Brian, Petrie Helen, Phipps Lawrie(2006), Contextual Web Accessibility – Maximizing the benefits of Accessibility Guidelines, *W4A at WWW2006. ACM 2006.*

Sodnik Jaka, Jakus Grega, Saso Tomazic (2010), Enhanced Synthesized Text Reader For Visually Impaired Users, IEEE Computer Society, 978-0-7695-3957-7/10 © 2010 IEEE.

Tsai Min-Jen (2006), VoiceXML dialog system of the multimodal IP-Telephony- The application for voice ordering service, Expert Systems and Applications 31(2006) 684-696 Elsevier.

Velasco Carlos A, Denev Dimitar, Stegemann Dirk, Mohamad Yehya (2008), *In W4A2008 – Communication Apr 21-22, 2008.*

Verma P., Singh R., Singh A. K., Yadav V., Pandey A.(2010), An Enhanced Speech-based Internet Browsing System for Visually Challenged", *In ICCCT 2010. DOI: 10.1109/ICCCT.2010.5640374*

Wang Hsin-min, Chen Berlin, Shen Liang-jui, and Chang Chao chi(2001), A Voice-Activated Web-based Mandarin Chinese Spoken Document Retrieval System.*ICCPOL2001.*

Yesilada Yeliz, and Harper Simon (2007), Web 2.0 and the Semantic Web: Hindrance or Opportunity? *In W4A- International Cross-Disciplinary Conference on Web Accessibility 2007.*

Yesilada Yeliz, Stevens Robert, Harper Simon and Goble Carole (2007),Evaluating DANTE: Semantic Transcoding for Visually Disabled Users, ACM Transactions on Human Computer Interaction, Vol.14, No. 3, Article 14, Sep 2007.

Yu Haibo, Mine Tsunenori, and Amamiya Makoto (2005), An Architecture for Personal Semantic Web Information Retrieval System- Integrating Web Services and Web Contents, In *Proceedings of the IEEE International Conference On Web Services (ICWS' 05)* IEEE Computer Society.

Yu Wai, McAllister Graham, Murphy Emma, Strain Philip, and McAllister Graham (2006), A novel multimodal interface for improving visually impaired people's web accessibility, Journal of Virtual Reality, Volume 9 Issue 2, January 2006.

Zajicek M., Powell C., and Reeves C.,(1999), Web search and orientation with Bookestalk, in *Proceedings of tech. and Persons with disabilities Conf., 1999.* Springer-Verlag London, UK

(II) WEB RESOURCES

Authoring Tool Accessibility Guidelines (ATAG) Overview [Internet]. dated 2008]. The World Wide Web Consortium; http://www.w3.org/WAI/intro/atag.php

Browse Aloud [http://www.browsealoud.com] Access on June 2012.

Document Object Model, [Internet]. http:// www.w3.org/DOM/[^] access date July, 2012.

EMACSPEAK,   access   date   March   2012 [http://emacspeak.sourceforge.net/smithsonian/study.html].

Enabling Dimensions, access date 2002[Internet]. Usage of Computers and Internet by the Visually Challenged: Issues and Challenges in the Indian context, Findings of a study conducted by Enabling Dimensions, January, 2002.

Evaluating Web Sites for Accessibility: Overview [Internet]. [updated 2009]. The World Wide Web Consortium; http://www.w3.org/WAI/eval/Overview.html

Freedom Scientific access date March 2012 [http://www.freedomscientific.com/] access on June, 2012.

How to Meet WCAG 2.0 [Internet]. [updated 2008]. The World Wide Web Consortium; http://www.w3.org/WAI/WCAG20/quickref

Internet Speech [http://www.internetspeech.com] access on June, 2012.

Java Speech, http://java.sun.com/products/java-media/speech/(accessed 22nd May, 2011).

Media Lab Asia [http://medialabasia.in/index.php/shruti-drishti]. Access on June 2012.

National Association For the Blinds [http://www.nabdelhi.org/NAB_SAFA.htm] Access on May 2012.

Practical   E-Commerce,   http://www.practicalecommerce.com/articles/2114-Screen-Readers-Eight-Frequently-Asked-Questions Access Date: July, 2012

SpeechML, http://www.alphaworks.ibm.com/formula/speechml. Access on June 2012.

TalkML, http://www.w3.org/Voice/TalkML/. Access on June 2012.

User Agent Accessibility Guidelines (UAAG) Overview [Internet]. [updated 2009]. The World Wide Web Consortium; http://www.w3.org/WAI/intro/uaag.html

VoiceXML, http://www.voicexml.org/. Access on June 2012.

VoXML, http://www.voxml.org/, Access on June 2012.

VoiceXML 2.0 http://www.w3.org/TR/voicexml20/(accessed March, 2011)

VoiceXML 2.1 http://www.w3.org/TR/voicexml21/(accessed 26th March, 2011)

WAI-ARIA Overview [Internet]. [updated 2009]. The World Wide Web Consortium; http://www.w3.org/WAI/intro/aria.php.

Web Accessibility Initiative (WAI) [Internet]. [updated 2010]. The World Wide Web Consortium (W3C); http://www.w3.org/WAI/,

WEBINSIGHT, accessed 2012, http://webinsight.cs.washington.edu/accessibility/.

W3C Voice Specification, Access Date March 2012, http://www.w3.org/Voice/.

W3C: Extensible Markup Language (2004) (XML) 1.0 (Third Edition), Feb 2004. http://www.w3.org/TR/2004/REC-xml-20040204/

(III) BOOKS

Markowitz J.,(1996). *Using Speech Recognition*, Prentice-Hall, NJ.

Cynthia, Shelly and George, Young(2006), *Writing Accessible Web Applications, Microsoft Accessibility Technology For Everyone,* 2006. Microsoft Press.

Schildt Herbert,(2010) *The Complete Reference C# 4.0*, Tata McGraw Hill.2010.

Stanislav Ondáš and Jozef Juhár(2010), *Development and Evaluation of the Spoken Dialogue System Based on the W3C Recommendations, Products and Services; from R&D to Final Solutions,* DOI: 10.5772/297, ISBN: 978-953-307-211-1.

Steinmetz R., and Nahrstedt K. (2004) *Multimedia Applications*, Springer.

LIST OF PUBLICATIONS
(OUT OF PRESENT RESEARCH WORK)

1. Verma Prabhat, Singh Raghuraj, Singh Avinash Kumar, (2012). A Framework for the Next Generation Screen Readers for Visually Challenged, published in International Journal of Computer Applications, Vol. 48, June 2012 Issue, ISBN: 978-93-80864-63-6, published by the Foundation of Computer Science, New York, USA.

2. Verma Prabhat, Singh Raghuraj,(2012) A Framework for Performance Evaluation of Internet Assistive Tools for Blind Users, accepted for publication in the IJCSIA (International Journal of Computer Science and its Applications) December Issue (Volume 2 Issue 3). Paper already presented at International Conference on Advances in Electronics, Electrical and Computer Science Engineering - EEC 2012.

3. Verma Prabhat, Singh Raghuraj, Singh Avinash Kumar, (2011). SICE: An Enhanced Framework for Design and Development of Speech Interfaces on Client Environment, published in International Journal of Computer Applications, Number 3 – Article 1, 2011. ISBN: 978-93-80864-63-6, published by the Foundation of Computer Science, New York, USA.

4. Verma Prabhat, Singh Raghuraj, Singh Avinash Kumar, Yadav Vibhash, Pandey Aditya,(2010) An Enhanced Speech based Internet Browsing System for Visually Challenged, *IEEE International Conference on Computer and Communication Technology (ICCCT-2010) at MNNIT, Allahabad during September, 17-19, 2010*, published in IEEExplore. ISBN: 978-1-4244-9033-2, DOI:10.1109/ICCCT.2010.5640374, Pages: 724-730.

5. Verma Prabhat, Singh Raghuraj, Singh Avinash Kumar, (2010) TC-GXML - A Transcoder for HTML to XML Grammar, *IEEE International Conference on Data Storage and Data Engineering (DSDE-2010) February 9-10, 2010, Bangalore, India*. Published in IEEE Computer Society, 978-0-7695-3958-4/10. DOI 10.1109/ DSDE.2010.69

6. Singh Raghuraj, Verma Prabhat, Singh Avinash Kumar, (2010) WACTA: A Speech-based Web Browser for Visually Challenged, *presented at Second IEEE International Conference on Intelligent Human Computer Interaction (IHCI-2010), January 16-18, 2010, IIIT, Allahabad*. Published by Springer.

7. Verma Prabhat, Singh Raghuraj, Singh Avinash Kumar, (2012) A Framework to Speech based Interface for Visually Disabled on the Websites of Public Interest", Communicated in *Human Centric Computing and Information Science,* A Springer Open International Journal. (Communicated Apr 16, 2012. Initial Assessment completed. Currently, Under Review).

Contact info: +91-9721456019, 9935654823
Prabhat Verma
Assistant Professor, Computer Science and Engineering Department,
Harcourt Butler Technological Institute, Kanpur-208002
E-mail : pvluk@yahoo.com

PRABHAT VERMA

PROFESSIONAL EXPERIENCE

- Currently, working as Asst. Professor in Computer Science and Engineering Department, Harcourt Butler Technological Institute, Kanpur Since 09.04.2003.
- Worked as Lecturer in MCA Department at V.B.S. Purvanchal University, Jaunpur from 28.05.2001 to 08.04.2003.
- 1.5 Years experience as JRF at IET, Lucknow.

ADMINISTRATIVE EXPERIENCE

- Worked as Joint Controller of Examination at HBTI, Kanpur from Apr 2009- 2012.
- Worked as Coordinator, HBTI- UPTU.
- Working as Hostel Warden, Lake-View since 2007.

ACADEMIC QUALIFICATIONS

- M. Tech. (Computer Science and Engineering) from Uttar Pradesh technical University, Lucknow in 2008 with CPI 9.67.
- B. E. in Computer Technology from Samrat Ashok Technological Institute, Barkatullah University, Bhopal in 1992 with 72% aggregate.
- Intermediate from M.P. Board, Bhopal, securing 75%(PCM), in 1988
- High School from from M.P. Board, Bhopal, securing 71% in 1986

M. TECH DISSERTATION

Topic: **"A Quality Assessment Model for Object-Oriented Software Systems"**
Guide: Prof. Raghuraj Singh, CSE Deptt., HBTI, Kanpur

AREA OF INTEREST

- Object oriented Systems
- Web Technology
- Artificial Intelligence

- Design and Analysis of Algorithms
- Operating Systems
- Data structure

PERSONAL INFORMATION

Name	:	PRABHAT VERMA
Date of Birth	:	21.06.1970.
Father's Name	:	Late Shri J. P. Verma
Sex	:	Male
Marital Status	:	Married
Address (Residence)	:	Type IV/D-5, East Campus,
		H.B.T.I., Nawabgunj, Kanpur-208002 (U.P.)

PRABHAT VERMA

www.ingramcontent.com/pod-product-compliance
Lightning Source LLC
La Vergne TN
LVHW092336060326
832902LV00008B/675